William Thompson Price

The technique of the drama

William Thompson Price

The technique of the drama

ISBN/EAN: 9783337303679

Printed in Europe, USA, Canada, Australia, Japan

Cover: Foto ©Paul-Georg Meister /pixelio.de

More available books at **www.hansebooks.com**

THE
TECHNIQUE
OF THE
DRAMA

A STATEMENT OF THE PRINCIPLES INVOLVED IN THE
VALUE OF DRAMATIC MATERIAL, IN THE
CONSTRUCTION OF PLAYS, AND IN
DRAMATIC CRITICISM

BY

W. T. PRICE

NEW YORK
BRENTANO'S
1905

PREFACE.

To set forth at any length in a preface the limitations and qualifications of mere rule and device in dramatic art, would be simply to anticipate the constant warnings against conventionalism and academic fixity that run through this book.

The vitality of the drama would soon be exhausted if writers followed rule only and were ignorant of principles or indifferent to them. It would be possible to describe with almost mathematical exactness how certain forms of the drama are built up, particularly those that are fixed or extinct; but it marks a decadence of the drama when at every step you are met with the mandate from the mechanical people—including prompter and scene-shifter—that you are to do this and are not to do that. The object of this book, then, is not to give formulas for the making of various kinds of plays, but to state such obvious and accepted principles as underlie the drama—principles that are known, or should be known, to every literary worker, and that are antecedent to the tricks of the trade. Succinctness is aimed at, but occasionally the exposition requires illustration.

Such few books of technique as are accessible in French and German seem to be impracticable in keeping too close to some special form, while English literature is completely lacking in helpful publications. The chief authority that a book of this kind can have is the authority of principle, and that only is urged for it.

This book is addressed not alone to the dramatic author, real or possible, but to the play-going public and the general student of literature as well, for there is inevitably a responsive elevation in the drama when audiences are critical enough to demand high work. To the dramatic critic of the newspaper the writer (having himself been in the living conflict) proffers the book as an aid in the ceaseless struggle against evil.

We have reached the beginning point of a

rapid development of the drama in America, and it is the hope of this writer—who lays no other store by it—that the book will be helpful, by way of suggestion if not of positive instruction, to honest and artistic work, to self-reliance and an independence of formula, to vigor in sentiment, purity in morals, and good taste.

W. T. PRICE.

NEW YORK, Nov., 1892.

SCHEDULE OF CHAPTERS.

CHAPTER		PAGE
I.	THE DRAMA．．．．．．．．．．．．．．．．．．．．．．．．．．．．．	1
	1. Its Definition; the Dramatic Idea.	
	2. The Use of the Drama.	
II.	THE THREE ELEMENTS OF A DRAMA．．．．．．．．	20
	1. The Ethical.	
	2. The Æsthetic.	
	3. The Technical.	
III.	THE PRINCIPLE OF UNITY．．．．．．．．．．．．．．．．．．	56
IV.	THE DIVISION INTO ACTS．．．．．．．．．．．．．．．．．．．	65

The Beginning { 1. The Introduction.
{ 2. The Development.

The Middle   3. The Crisis or Climax.

The End { 4. The Denouement.
{ 5. The Catastrophe.

V.	THE SCENES AND PRINCIPLES OF ACTION．．．．．	112
	1. Monologues.	
	2. Dialogues.	
	3. Groups.	
	4. Masses.	
	Etc.	
VI.	CHARACTER ．．．．．．．．．．．．．．．．．．．．．．．．．．．．．．	149
VII.	A SUMMARY OF CERTAIN LAWS IN ART ．．．．．．	165
	1. Perspicuity.	
	2. Proportion.	
	3. Variety.	
	4. Illusion.	
	5. Probability.	
	6. Contrast.	
	Etc.	

CHAPTER		PAGE
VIII.	ADAPTATION AND DRAMATIZATION	178
IX.	FORMS OF THE DRAMA	191
X.	CRITICISM	212
XI.	HOW A DRAMA IS BUILT UP: A WORD TO THE AUTHOR	224
XII.	THE LITERATURE OF DRAMATIC PRINCIPLE	243

THE TECHNIQUE OF THE DRAMA.

CHAPTER I.

THE DRAMA.

1. DEFINITION.—A drama is the imitation of a complete action, adapted to the sympathetic attention of man, developed in a succession of continuously interesting and continuously related incidents, acted and expressed by means of speech and the symbols, actualities, and conditions of life.

No definition in a paragraph, however comprehensive in terms, of what a drama is, can more than indicate its limitations and proportions. For the unskilled in particular, large elucidation is necessary to bring out the hidden meaning of the above descriptive phrases. The definition as given concerns itself largely with the form of a play, including the general dramatic idea. It is obvious that the fitness of material for the form must be governed by the requirements of a drama; and this definition affords an absolute rule of measurement.

The drama in general is a reflex of life. The truth of this is to be found in the literature of any people, for in this form in proportion to its development at any given period, more than in any other form, are embodied sentiment and manners. The playwright may treat his theme as he may, with idealism or realism, and there yet remains in his work something of his time. It is for this reason that dramas are so perishable. Changes of taste and manners work this ruin. The commercial author cares more for this adaptability in his piece than for any of its other qualities. The drama deals with men. It requires spectators, and is addressed to the eye, the ear, and the moral nature. It is a form of literature and of entertainment into which all human emotions and experience may be translated under certain conditions. That idea only is dramatic that can be put into shape of sustained action—an action that is complete and organic, with unity of theme and purpose, that invites our attention at the outset, arouses an interest as it proceeds, and confirms itself in our sympathies at the last, coming to a conclusion in its disposition of the characters that accords with our views of justice. Only a vital and logical action can do this. An action is complete —according to the first requirement—when everything essential to its sympathetic appreciation is contained in it. There is, of course, a vast knowledge of life, particular as well as general to any theme that may be chosen, that is implied in the action as possessed by the spectator, and this, the unexpressed, is a material source of one's enjoyment, giving play to our emotion and intelligence.

As stated by Aristotle, a complete action is one that has a beginning, a middle, and an end; or, as it may be put, it contains a premise, an argument, and a conclusion. The premise or the beginning is a fact or state of facts, undisputed, accepted; for the action must have a sure starting-point. No antecedents, at least in the way of action, are required to explain it.

Shakspere tells, for example, in "Romeo and Juliet" nothing of the causes or former incidents of quarrel between the Montagues and the Capulets. It is a sufficient beginning that the two houses are at deadly enmity. We see from this how the law of limitation at once asserts itself. Every form of art has its boundaries, and in this dogma of a beginning we touch the first sure dramatic ground. In the play in question the theme is love, not politics or history. The middle is the development from the premise or fact, which has necessarily preceded it, and which just as necessarily requires a deduction or conclusion. The end leaves nothing more to be said or done. A result, the consequence of what has preceded, is reached.

The drama is practical—truth being its essence —growing more and more so as it deals with the complex relations of modern society; consequently themes at this day are by preference and custom not handled in verse, and even the elocution that attends the Shaksperian dramas is uttered in tones and a rhythm truer to nature than in the times of Siddons and Kemble. The drama is concrete. It is not only life, but the essence of it, the selection and use of those things only that tend to illusion. It puts aside reflection, the elegiac, the lyric, the merely descriptive, except as they are briefly incidental, and translates all into action. It holds all forms of literature and all things of life in solution, but on the condition of adapted form and that they be integral with the action and the purpose. The drama is a powerful solvent and can make many things "dramatic" that in themselves are not so, but become so when vital and in place.

Certain things, as will better appear than in

this chapter, must be dramatic. The theme must be dramatic, else it will not admit of the development indicated in the rule. The heart of the dramatic is emotion and that action which springs from or leads to a clash of personal interests that by incertitude of incident proceeds to a final result. The Divine law, social and political conditions, are the higher causes in this movement. The drama is a conflict always. The problem is always to remove an obstacle. Dramatic are the emotions that give shape to will and deed. All emotions, all events that involve logical destiny (or in comedy artificial destiny) to the person or persons concerned, are dramatic. There is a drama in every throb of the human heart. It requires the clash of interests to make a complete action. It matters not what force impels. Desire and demand, opposition, resistance, the thrust and the parry, and so through vicissitudes to joy or grief.

An idea for practical purposes is not dramatic unless it can be acted in all its material parts. It may be in the nature of the dramatic, and in the way of description may make a striking poem like "Sheridan's Ride" or "Hervé Riel."

An epic poem may describe great deeds. The novelist and the lyric poet may tell of emotion, but in the drama it is the actor alone that is entitled to speak ; and, even in the best technically written drama, every device or subterfuge, however necessary, that shows the hand or the mind of the author, is a defect. Description by an actor, on the other hand, may be highly dramatic. An incident may be more effectively acted by means of it than if it had been represented, possibly tediously, before us.

The play is moreover to be acted in a given time. This is one of its many limitations. Three hours is a high limit of comfort and convenience in a theatre, but apart from this practical experience, a drama expanded beyond this space is in danger of wearying either by monotony or by variety and multiplicity of incidents. Three thousand lines is given as the proper length of a play. A safer estimate is the time consumed in reading the manuscript aloud, with an allowance for the business, the general affairs of the stage, and the intervals between the acts.

The dramatic idea must be susceptible of division into proportionate parts. Its beginning, middle, and end must have absolute relations. Causes and effects must be adequate. A trivial ending must not result from a serious progression of incidents. The beginning, the middle, and the end should be relatively proportionate in treatment.

The dramatic idea involves a general theme, such as love, jealousy, ambition, nobility of nature; and a particular theme, such as the love of Romeo and Juliet, and so on.

It involves an object, such as to show that love is stronger than the world and all its laws. To abstract from a play other incidental themes and objects would be to deny it human semblance. Themes are simple or complex, but unity is the governing rule in either case.

The dramatic idea should be based on the truth of life, and thus probability is an essential thing.

The theme is of the first importance, for no genuine play was ever written without the process of germination in the heart and mind of a writer. "The choice of subject" is not a happy phrase. It is true that the value of the material must be determined; and to this end is definition herein made of the dramatic idea. It is worth while to add that particular themes are often found by a playwright to be practically exhausted for his generation. Of course, general themes—love, jealousy, and the like—offer boundless complications. Certain combinations of condition are intensely dramatic at certain social periods, but as soon as the social conditions no longer concern us, they cease to be of interest.

Action in itself, emotion in itself, is not necessarily dramatic. It is only so when organic with larger action, or when complete in itself. There are plays which are not dramatic, and yet which contain perfect dramas in this or that incident, which may concern characters that have little or nothing to do with the main action. A case in point is where in the course of the action of a pretentious play a Vendean peasant is slain, and bewailed by his wife—ten minutes of real drama to three hours of meandering.

Emotion without cause given may appear absurd. If we are not made to sympathize with it and understand it, we resent it as an obtrusion. In other words, it may be a futile theatre trick and not dramatic. Mere movement may become a tedious insult to people who give their money, time, and attention to a performance. Play-botchers, the conventional thieves of the stage, pilfer climaxes from honest dramas and construct pieces that are not true plays. Battle, murder, and sudden death, the uplifted knife and the deadly bowl, are under such conditions not tragic or dramatic, but the figments of uninformed trickery, theatric merely.

In its proper place a given situation may have a powerful effect, but the governing principle is that it must be organic.

The definition of a drama does not prescribe intensity for the dramatic idea or the chief situation. To do so would be to define a particular form of the drama only. If you have the conditions of an action, the cause, the effects, and finality, the dramatic idea is complete. It is true that certain incidents are in themselves dramatic because the mind supplies the qualities just indicated, as if we were to witness the burning of a city, but the effect is only momentary. If that city be Moscow, in whose flames the prestige of Napoleon is destroyed, the interest is quickened. It becomes a part of a larger drama. The spectacle of the assassination of a man, or of the beheading of a woman, would give no other sensation than of horror; but when we know with all material circumstance that the one is Marat and the other Marie Antoinette, we feel at once the force of the dramatic idea— an idea that may be developed with curiosity, interest, suspense, and emotion; but we need not go so far afield for illustration, inasmuch as the ordinary tragedies and happenings of life interest us and are dramatic in proportion to our personal knowledge of the facts and the people involved. Even then the story or the plot must excite natural sympathy.

The dramatic idea, then, cannot exist apart in

the mind, and with all the more reason cannot stand unsupported on the stage, consisting of a single act or doing.

The dramatic idea involves incidents, and these incidents lie about it in greater or less profusion. Emotion is full of action; and the idea is dramatic in proportion to the emotion it excites in the spectator of the scene compounded of it. It is so in real life. A dramatic happening unfolds itself from these emotions step by step, link by link.

We must have an origin for each incident, and an expectation of results. It does not need to conceive mortal peril or death in order to be dramatic. The dramatic principle includes all human action. These incidents may be so highly charged with the dramatic that they may be almost perfect in themselves, but in the true drama it is the entirety alone that is "a complete action." The drama itself is not complete until it is acted, and its possibilities have been expressed in action, utterance, look, tone, and gesture.

A complete action is in itself a definition of unity, one of the essentials.

So organic is the dramatic idea, that any of its parts, a subordinate incident even, may become in the mind of the poet the germ of the play. Schiller reads a paragraph of a few lines in a paper, telling of the suicide of two lovers of unequal birth; and from that springs his "Cabale und Liebe."

Sardou sees a piece of paper blown out of a window, and that is the beginning of his wonderfully written "Pattes de Mouches." The dramatic idea may be weighed in advance of its treatment by the incidents it suggests. Does it admit of handling like a case at law, where all but particular evidence is excluded? A trial is a drama if it reaches a conclusion, acquittal, or conviction, with an element the while of uncertainty as to result. It is this uncertainty, this suspense, as it is technically called, that is implied in the "sympathetic attention" of the definition of the drama already given.

By way of familiar illustration, it may be said that a perfect anecdote possesses many of the essential features of a drama. It is always a complete action. The local anecdote, in particular, admits of great detail in the telling. The persons concerned in it are known, as are their relations to each other. It has a beginning, an introduction, a climax, and a conclusion, and that conclusion leaves nothing more to be said or done. The more conclusive, the more the village will roar its applause. The adaptability of the anecdote to practical stage use explains the prosperity of the American farce-comedies. A farce-comedy is little more than a succession of acted anecdotes.

Progressive action is a true mark of the dramatic product, and if there is not a propelling force in the incidents that lie about a theme it is not dramatic. Progression toward an end is essential.

The material of the drama lies about us and is common property, often enough in forms requiring small technical shaping. Actual happenings furnish a large part of it, so that "originality" is not one of the most desired merits of a dramatic author. He may be accounted original because of the use or even invention of some situation not before seen in the drama, but, after all, it is we, the people, to whom that situation is possible in real life, or who may in hard fact have acted it, that are the real authors of plays. Millions of men ceaselessly co-operate with the dramatist. The real power and merit of an author have ample scope in truly telling what passes in the human heart. A genuine drama is the distillation of his life, fancy, meditation, and all the genius of his being. The commonplaces of life are pregnant with drama.

"Originality" is usually but another name for

The Drama.

artificiality, marking the point of departure from simple nature and everyday life. W. S. Gilbert is original in the " Mikado "; and in farce, which does not confine itself to reality, there may be any amount of caprice. The true drama is bounded on all sides by fact. Life, and the life that he knows, is the best material for any honest-minded dramatist. There is where spontaneity lies. There are other sources of the drama, notably history and romance, and from these the author may draw and be absolutely original. There are difficulties in dealing with history. A drama has a direct growth in the mind and heart of a writer, and the less he is encumbered with non-essential incidents and incidentals, the easier his task. In historical material he may disentangle himself, but he will be met on the production of the piece by these same non-essentials existent in the minds of the audience. It is much the same with dramatizations of novels or incidents suggested by them. The difficulties in either case will be discussed in the technical chapters. The dramatic idea may sometimes be stronger than history itself.

The material of the drama may come from any life, but it is a sure indication of a rogue when he writes only foreign plays. It is these mental *sans-culottes*, these adapters and thieves, that stultify managers and intercept good, genuine work. Our stage and our literature are vastly concerned in this. Let the managers look to home work with more faith. The history of its financial success even in the present development of our drama is convincing as to its value.* It is odd how original work is mistrusted by the merchants in the temple, and yet nothing is more certain than that each country reserves its heartiest welcome for the home product.

Yet, it certainly matters not where a play comes from. The stage is universal, and the imprints of London, Paris, Germany, are indifferent, if we accept them. But it does make a difference who writes the plays. A French play should be written by a Frenchman, an English play by an Englishman, and a German play by a German. You can't make anything else out of a native writer of foreign plays except a cheap imitator.

It is true that Shakspere made large choice of foreign material, but exclusive of his mastery and the ampler treatment allowed by the technique of his day, the propriety of its use is

---

* " My Partner," " The Danites," " Davy Crockett," " The White Slave," " The Banker's Daughter," " Shenandoah," " Held by the Enemy," "Alabama," etc. ; while England will have nothing that is not English by origin or adaptation.

The Drama.

entirely sound. His was the poetic drama. It has the freedom of the world. He treated history and fable where the essential facts are fixed, or, on occasion, of obscure countries like Denmark and Bohemia, as to which he could establish conditions. He was, moreover, true in his vision. At all events, there is reason to be very, very suspicious of any American drama on a foreign theme of current life. There is power and truth in the native theme. The Frenchmen are great because of their loyalty; because they write home plays.

Wherever the theme, or, in other words, the dramatic idea, may come from, it has certain inherent rights; it first stirs the heart and hand of the writer to action, and to it is given dominion and power over the technique to be applied to it. It demands and suggests its own treatment, and an author should take careful counsel with it before yielding to conventionalism, when the idea finds its opposition there.

Technique is the helper; the subject is the master. The man with an idea is more fortunate than the one with the tools; and yet perfection is the requirement of the drama, and to it the dramatist must bend his will. The artificialities of play-writers are not fixed, but the principles are inexorable. Of course the general requirements of a drama as stated in this chapter involve other principles, and these we shall encounter as we proceed.

2. THE USE OF THE DRAMA.—Holding fast to the principle that the drama is life, we must see that its uses are noble. There are many forms of the drama, and some whose graceless mission is to corrupt; so that it is the variety of the drama that brings so much confusion into all talk of it. The value of the drama is not to be seriously disputed for a moment. It is essential in many ways to civilization. In large cities, where the physical congregation is social segregation, it takes the place to a certain extent of the social and moral influences that are active in the compact life of smaller communities.

It is only worth while, in a book devoted to the art of building plays, to speak of this particular matter in a practical way. Dramatic literature, with its English charter from Shakspere, can take care of itself.

A pernicious theory is held by some managers and writers, that the purpose of the drama is merely <u>to entertain</u>.

So should a sermon entertain, and have art after its kind, too. A drama must certainly entertain, or it fails; but it is a shallow assumption that proclaims that as its only function.

Were it the case, we should have every indecency exhibited, whereas the drama should minister to the heart. This would soon outlaw the art. Were it the only function, it would be a miserable life-pursuit for the people of genius, of dignity, and moral grandeur that walk in the ranks of the stage, honored and worthy. If to amuse were all, then we should have clowns only. A serious and entertaining drama cannot help but instruct. It is a supplement to our life. Its potentialities are not to be doubted. Its molding influence cannot be weighed, but it exists. We know that it can affect the moral and political life of a nation. It would be easy to give examples without recurring to the time when in Greece the drama was national. And, so, the drama acts on individuals, and results are hidden in the multitude of hearts. The slightest examination into the principles of the drama proves that no successful and well-constructed drama can preach and teach at the public. It is not its way of handling the material, but the sermon and the lesson will be there just as truly.

Moreover, people are not entertained by provocation of laughter alone. It is a catch-word with the commercial manager, that "people go to the theatre to laugh." If this were true, every definition of the dramatic idea is at fault. In point of fact a play is directed at the emotions of people, and laughter is but one of the many. Another catch-word in the same relation is that "people don't want to think." This statement proceeds from small knowledge of the dramatic process of construction. A good play —"Richard III.," or what-not—is plain sailing for the lads in the gallery, and is without distressful mental operation for anybody.

Of all the arts the drama comes closest to man. It dwells with him. It does not deal mainly with the gods, as mute statuary does, and is not sightless and impalpable, like music. It does not halt at the single moment, as painting does. It embraces all the arts, and gives life and voice and form and functions to them all. No other art uses such a multiplicity of forces.

Imagine the cost of some single, great dramatic production, and what in the end it brings to author, actor, and manager.

Let us say that it earns a quarter of a million dollars; and men everywhere that have beheld it carry with them memories for life, for they have seen something done by men, not marble, and have beheld pictures painted by passion and life, not by pigments. Their experiences have been enlarged, for man is made of dreams. Perspectives have been opened up that are new to some minds, and to them, otherwise, impossible. It teaches wisdom to men that never open a book. It gives the essence of life, and in three hours it speaks volumes. It warns and counsels, teaches justice and keeps alive pity. It celebrates man's liberty and his struggles, and all that is noble wanders into it. It enlists the sympathies to such an extent that the listener is his own poet. It analyzes all motives, withholding nothing, lays bare everything. It is in fact the plainest, the most direct of all forms of teaching. It does not formulate morals in words, but in deeds; and if life, which is the drama, is not a constant mentor, unheeded also in its teachings, what is it?

CHAPTER II.

THE THREE ELEMENTS OF A DRAMA.

WE are still considering the dramatic idea—the theme. The poet must determine in advance of putting his hand to it what its qualities are. Is it worth his while to put it into form? It is a matter of labor, and he must look to results. There are three elements in the dramatic idea: the ethical, the æsthetic, and the technical; and deficiency in any one of them may make the entire material inapt.

1. THE ETHICAL.—The theme, with its facts and what is proved in the conclusion of the drama, must accord with the moral views of the time in which the drama is produced. In the lighter forms of comedy there is no ethical purpose, although the play may be even more iniquitous than if it had a bad purpose, or, on the other hand, more effective than if the problem were openly set. Every play leaves an impression, and that impression must be taken as its object. In the serious drama it is impossible to

avoid the issue of morals, and in many modern pieces a social question is avowedly discussed. Dumas in "Denise"* seeks to establish the proposition that a girl who becomes a mother out of wedlock may be entirely innocent. Whatever may be said in behalf of this child of misfortune, her case is not for the drama under our social code. There is an object in every drama. That object is the one distinct thing in the poet's mind and heart from the beginning, long before he passes through the incertitudes of the technical handling and reaches the heart of the drama, so that it assuredly must be absolutely distinct when he has completed his work. An immoral incident in a play may pass without resistance, but an immoral object is fatal. This fundamental rule is plain enough, but great treasure is lavished on plays of the kind that inevitably fail, and the genius of actors is thrown away on them. The authority of some author who is technically great is often the mis-

* The plays cited in this book are used only by way of illustration, and not necessarily because of merit. Care has been taken to refer to familiar plays, or to such as are accessible, particularly in French's edition of "The Standard Drama," or in other printed form. The play that serves for illustration is immaterial. The very latest play will reveal to you no new principles, however well it may serve to illustrate the same principles that are common to the drama of all time and all lands.

leading factor. We have also to reckon with the fatuous daring of some actor whose judgment has gone astray on artificialities. It is because of the fact that the public encounters these plays, in spite of plain, common sense, that a discussion is here demanded in a book of technique.

Let us consider "Renée de Moray," as is entitled one of the versions of "Martyr," by D'Ennery. It goes beyond the limit of all forbearance. It is immoral, repulsive—and, naturally, illogical. The piece has succumbed to the scorn of every English-speaking public. It failed in London. It may have had a measure of success in Paris, where a certain social theory holds that one's grandmother may bear an illegitimate child with disgrace dependent only on the fact becoming known. The implication is that such occurrences are not uncommon, and that there is a romantic piquancy about the intrigue. When such a history is transferred to the English stage, there is a monstrous something in it that touches every household in the land.

It is not a question of "morals" in the way of exciting the imagination, for it is too odious for that. Nor is it the mere theme in itself. Vice, as depicted on the stage, becomes dangerous only when that vice goes unpunished. In "Renée" there is not the slightest suggestion of a reprimand. We all know "Frou Frou," in which a most lovable creature of whim and fashion endures a fate that reconciles us to her for her misfortunes, whereby she pays in full the harsh score of humanity. "Camille," or "Heart's-ease" as it is sometimes called, is of similar quality, and no one can withhold from this figure of fiction, so true to the facts of life as ideally stated, the forgiveness that she craves in parting with a world unhappy for her. We sympathize with her in "The New Magdalen." We take sides in "Forget-Me-Not." We weep with Miss Multon, and in its prototype "The Stranger" we confess a pity for Mrs. Haller. There is, then, a wide distinction between such plays and "Mme. Renée de Moray."

This drama is of a most extraordinary nature. There are Greek plays, plays of genius, that are full of power and based on ideas of similar horror, but it is acknowledged that in them there is an element of fate not understood in any modern religion or social theory.

A drama must deal with accepted facts or definitely prove a given proposition. It may take a theme that is open to discussion, but if it fails to gain the consent of the listener to certain human actualities, it is not a drama. D'Ennery's fundamental idea may be an accepted thing in France, to wit, that one's grandmother may have had an intrigue in her youth, that she may marry a man—whom she may or may not love—be distinguished for good qualities, held in devotion by her family, and be in every way a model *mère*. She may irradiate the room with her saintliness when she is about. She is blameless if her son, the ante-nuptial, as a toddler has escaped her vigilance and gone off into space, to grow up and return as a vigorous blackmailer of his half-sister. She has only to express a tear and the son forgives her. A daughter may sacrifice her own happiness, consent to separation from her own husband, see him married to an adventuress, be parted from her child, witness her husband brutally murder a man, her half-brother, on the warrant of her own lie—in short, disgrace herself and everybody else—to what purpose? In the end she explains to everybody, including, at the outset of the denouement, her innocent daughter and her own mother. The good old man, her father, considerately dies before her revelation, but the incident seems to be of small importance in the American versions of the play, for no tears are shed; only it may be assumed that the old

The Three Elements of a Drama. 25

admiral, as a distinguished officer, was followed to Père la Chaise with discreet desolation.

Does the mother of Renée suffer? Not at all. Does, in fact, Renée herself experience any particular discomfort in her "martyrdom"? She retires temporarily with a dower, rich enough to save her husband from ruin in the end, when she comes to his rescue and falls into his arms after he had procured a divorce from the adventuress. Her husband had committed bigamy in marrying the female garlic-eater from Naples, anyway. This adventuress has known the secret all the while, and retires with complacency when she sees that the crime of the original sinner is known to all the world. What nonsense, putrid nonsense, it all is! A woman, who is a grandmother, has the secret as to her illegitimate child protected by her daughter, under circumstances of misery, and retains the custody of that daughter's innocent daughter!

Again we find an English play, "Harvest," wherein the author takes up the wrongs of a wife and varnishes over a semi-tragedy of life with comedy, working filigree on fustian of his own.

It is not up to the common measure of sympathy. A husband abandons the wife of his youth on a pitiful pretext suggested by a devil in broadcloth, backed by an impertinent law book, and, twenty years later, when both are blighted by old age, he re-marries his despoiled victim. We are required to believe that a real man would so act and should so act, but we are constrained to think that such morals and such imbecility of will and heart could only exist in a character made up of theatrical moonshine. Pitiful indeed is the case of the women of England if cold abandonment and wandering lust are within the scheme of aristocratic life and permissible to his lordship. It is not sound morals, and a play based on such motives is of no avail. The upshot of a serious play is always moral, or there is no play, and the processes of action must be genuine and not a trick. The love of the woman is not a strong enough antiseptic to the baseness of the hero in the case cited. Artifice defeats itself. Again we find the resources of a theatre devoted to a play, "The Mousetrap," in which sympathetic attention is sought for the woman that poisons her husband.

The drama may and must handle incidents of great moral delicacy, but the general purpose is the test of purity: crime, for that matter, is one of the foundations of the drama. It is not, for example, a question of morals in Sardou's "La Tosca," but of taste; and the two are often confounded in criticism. In "Measure for Measure" there is a moment of wavering virtue on the part of Isabella's brother. In "Cymbeline," Iachimo comes from Italy in a most repellent character. In "Fazio" the heroine confronts peril to her chastity.

Everywhere in the drama we meet with delicate situations, but the test is always the purpose, or, better put, the effect of the play. More than this, there is an indefinable something in the writings of a man that declares his purity of heart or his real lack of reverence for virtue; and so the satyr peeps out of much that Goethe wrote, although his Gretchen in "Faust" has furnished the most truly moral piece that our stage knows.

Moral prejudice may at times be false, and opinions may change. Moral principle may likewise waver, but the rule given will hold in its practical bearings. In the Roman Coliseum it was sport to witness men torn by tigers. We have only to examine the notions of virtue in the old English comedies of manner to see that a book of dramatic technique cannot attempt to establish moral laws, and yet the rule holds, for every man must write in the spirit of his age in order to get acceptance; and that age sets up its own principles of right and wrong.

Reference has been made to the fact that formal teaching and preaching is impossible in the drama, but that the lesson and the sermon are, notwithstanding, contained in the drama. To excite discussion and opposition in the mind of the spectator is against a fundamental principle. The poet must gain the full consenting attention of his audience from the outset, and firmly hold it, or he can never establish the illusion that is the chief triumph of a play. If the listener cannot dispute your moral proposition, or is strong in his belief in it, it remains simply a question of embodying it in agreeable and dramatic shape. You are not going to get his laughter, his tears, and his applause by "eloquence," argument, and literary gems distributed among characters in a play; but if these characters are true to life they may gain these tributes by the simple processes of the drama. Truth and actuality vanish from a drama when the author usurps the functions of the persons of the play. The characters become mechanical, the play creaks with clumsy structure. A play has such peculiar coherency that the moral gets expression not only in the sum of all the action—the impression left by it—but in detail of character, conversation, and incident.

The law of contrast, as well as the law of variety, requires that vice be very often portrayed. The Bible teaches virtue by the same method. This coincidence happens because both Bible and Drama concern humanity and its weaknesses.

Comedy is not subject to the severe judgment that is applied to the serious forms of the drama. Where the object of a play is mere amusement, the spectator does not make its morals a personal matter, because, as a rule, the fable is not supposed to teach anything. But the license of comedy should not be permitted to go too far, and to fight indecency and immorality should be held as one of the most solemn obligations of the press.

As a matter of fact, and purely in its business aspect, there is no lasting gain or popularity in an immoral play, however encouraging results may be at its production.

2. THE ÆSTHETIC.—The matter of taste is bound up in every drama, and it will always have disputed boundaries; but to offend taste in the theme, or in any dominant part of it, is fatal

to a drama. It is meant to include in this division of the dramatic essentials; and in the word æsthetic, the quality of entertainment. A play is directed to the eye and the ear, and to the intelligence and the heart. It must entertain. It can best do so when it is safely built in morals, taste, and technical form. Goethe has very truly said somewhere that some of the ablest men, writers who are instructive and have something to tell, utterly lack the power of entertaining. This element of entertainment must exist in a drama, therefore entertainment is the object of play-writing. "Acceptability" more nearly expresses this element than either "the æsthetic" or "the quality of entertainment." Thus we do not accept Tolstoi's "Kreutzer Sonata," because it offends the joys and tender relations of life. It is a powerful story, yet soon or late, during or after examining it, we reject it. Its intent is certainly not immoral; on the contrary, deeply religious; and the interest is morbid rather than entertaining.

It is not absolutely needful, in order to entertain, that a play should excite laughter, even in passages. The subject may not admit of it, and many great and absorbing plays have not a jot of humor in them.

Laughter is only one form of acceptability.

The distinction between pleasure or delight in a thing and laughter is very plainly set forth in Sir Philip Sidney's treatise, "An Apology for Poetry," known also as "The Defense of Poesy." "We delight in good chances, we laugh at mischances."

All that sustains interest and excites emotion brings the action within the rule. It is a miserable device, when used merely as a device, to have scenes at intervals for the stock comedian. We shall see that variety is a rule, and we may be sure that an intelligent author will find what humor for the purpose lies in the material he handles. Dryden attempted to write a play on the principle of tempering a complete tragedy with a complete comedy, and failed.

Taste may be offended by the offense of morals in the manner already pointed out. On the other hand, a play may be absolutely correct in that particular, and yet its theme be monstrous. The spectacle of a murderer besieging the heart of his victim's daughter is surely not pleasing, and yet the subject is not unknown.

Possibly a theory may exist that the public must take care of itself in matters of taste, and that art and its proper limitations are determined only by the receipts at the door of a theatre. It may be urged in defense of the lover in quest of his victim's daughter, that the Greek dramatists abound in horrors, that the incest of Œdipus was to them a powerful theme; but these fables are based on a mythology and a system of life dominated by fate, all of which is not at present fully understood. Victor Hugo has brought within the limits of art "the last day of a condemned," and Goethe has followed the processes of emotion that brought Werther to self-destruction. These were psychological studies, pursued by genius during a morbid period of literary production. In seizing upon themes of a like nature, the modern dramatist is far afield, wandering off, like the Sarcelites once did, into "a land of devils and hogs." An unacted play has sought production among managers, in which the hero, a divine youth, falls in love with the daughter of the man he has murdered, and finally swelters in his accomplished desire. In Corneille's "Cid" there is something of the sort. It is, however, of a different quality. Possibly "Fedora" may have turned endeavor thitherward. The variance between Sardou's play and these products is essentially wide. There is no domestic life in "Fedora," no fond father, no babbling uncle with his heart a-flutter with goodness, no prattling children, no home desecrated.

"Fedora" is the true growth out of conditions that lead to passion and to crime—both unrestrained, both in a manner justified—and for theatrical purposes, entirely so. It may be remarked that we view certain actions with toleration, even with great interest, only because the *dramatis personæ* are entirely foreign to our own national life.

To illustrate how ruinously works an idea, if fundamental to the play and in bad taste, let us take an example. Thus runs the story: An old gambler, broken in fortune, still pursuing his luck at the gaming-tables of Paris, lives in a modest retreat in that great city. In an altercation about a note that he holds against a young man, that person, who passes under an assumed name, stabs him with a fruit knife, and fatally. The lover of the old man's daughter finds him dying, and to the scrawling accusation written by the failing fingers he adds at dictation the name of the murderer — the assumed name. Gwynne, the daughter, swears to avenge her father's murder. She is adopted by a friend of her father, and is made co-heir of his estate with his nephew. This nephew is the murderer. He attempts to throw suspicion on the true lover in order to get him out of the way and marry the girl. He urges his suit. He is finally exposed.

The element of suspense in the action is entirely lacking. Suspense—the technical meaning of which the author doubtless understands—is bound up in our sympathy with the characters of a play—the suspense being completed by our curiosity as to the result of the action, step by step. It is an absolute element. Action is made up of opposing forces.

The clash is felt and the flash is evoked only when the metal of the combatants is of equal temper. The villain's advantages and his resources for evil must be formidable. We must have a certain respect for him. He must have a natural motive, one that may at least be understood. Mere mechanism will not do. As before indicated, suspense begins only with interest in the action. At what point does interest attach to this plot? We know that the girl is in no danger of falling in love with the murderer. The audience would not forgive her, at any rate. We can't believe in the sincerity of his love. We wouldn't tolerate it if we could. We are not beguiled.

We foresee a shame that must come over the house of Gwynne's benefactor in the hanging of his nephew. Much of the machinery of the play is in consequence preposterous. Unless the premises of an action are accepted, a drama is futile. The play comes too close home to the English sense of domestic life.

It can't be repeated too often, that "The Harvests," "The Mousetraps," and plays of the kind just mentioned, are not and cannot be dramas, it matters not what skill is applied to them, or what amount of money is spent on them; and the technical faults, as pointed out before, are proof that the form is faulty or lifeless where the material is bad to begin with. It is trying to make a silk purse out of a sow's ear.

The technical part in the three plays described was good enough, but what they set forth is not acceptable. It is not realism. It is not romance. It is pernicious, not in teaching a bad moral—for it has none—but in the matter of taste and reason.

The conditions of the drama are so peculiar that even the villain must be admirable in his creation and give entertainment in the acting. Surely Hamlet's uncle is not worse than that female character, the poisoner, in "The Mousetrap"; Gwynne's lover is not more reprehensible than Richard III. It is a question of taste in the dramatist's use of the poisoners and murderers—those worthies of the drama.

It is true that there is nothing in literature so strongly marked as the changes in taste. Charles

Surface, when he came from Sheridan's hand, was a generous and dashing blade, as appears from the recurring type in other plays of the day. We regard him now as a dissolute reprobate. Othello as a sooty African is not possible with some audiences. Taste is not wholly a matter of philosophic right or wrong.

Prejudice dictates its terms to the drama. In a practical sense it is folly to combat it unless you are in the right, and conduct the case skillfully, securing toleration, then interest, and finally agreement with your proposition. Lessing has done this in "Nathan the Wise," a plea for the brotherhood of man in relation with the Jew. In a play of these latter days, on the contrary, a social iniquity bursts on the startled hearers at the end of the first act, and sends the hero through his trials as a bastard. It is a fatal dramatic error. The result is that a subordinate character in the piece sends Philip, the illegitimate gentleman, to the rear, and becomes the real hero. In another play, one of the two rival lovers, comrades, betrays the other, represents to the girl that the other, the favored one, has been killed in war, and so succeeds in marrying her. A child is born. The true and honorable lover returns. There is a scene. The true-blue lover, vanquished by the baby, departs. The husband goes away and redeems himself in battle, and, somehow, restores himself to honor and the love and respect of his wife. Pieced out with comedy, this action makes the play. It is in bad taste, and consequently undramatic from beginning to end. We must always reckon the upshot of a drama and the effects in it as in the purpose of the author.

In the case of the bastard as the principal character in a play, we have a defiance of prejudice. The clash is with the audience, not between the elements of the play. Distinguished historical characters, subjects of the drama, have irregularity of lineage, but the matter of taste is not involved. It is the wrong application of a fact that damages the material. In "Harvest" the brutality of the husband, who defers justice beyond the day of youth, outrages the forbearance of all true hearts. The instinct of the universal fist is against him.

The exigencies of the plot and the prevailing abundance of other features may reduce distasteful points to harmless proportions. Claude Melnotte is a licensed peddler of lies, beginning his love-suit in infamy and returning at the close as one of the scoundrels who made fortunes in pillaging Italy under the Directory; but the events of the play condone it all, somehow.

The Raphaelesque theory that art is to concern itself with beauty only, is not applicable to the whole wide domain of the drama. The idealist has his share only as a creator of plays. The theme should, of course, be worthy of attention. The madness of Cora in "Article 47" is in no wise a beautiful spectacle, but the emotion is touched and refined rather than offended. The scene of a woman dying in a paroxysm of poisoning is not an æsthetic thing, nor is the play of "The Sphinx," in which it occurs, of durable popularity, but it is within the field of art.

The Greek canon would never permit the scenes of death that are so common on our stage. We accept the portrayal of life without abating any of its tragedy; good taste drawing the line beween the truly dramatic and the merely theatric and realistic; the heart responding to the one, the mind despising the other.

Art is to produce effects, and the art applied to a bad purpose may be as precise and powerful as that applied to a good; but, on the whole, good acting can never redeem bad taste.

It is not within the design of this book to treat of the philosophy of taste. Volumes on æsthetics exist in abundance, but taste is of little practical use to a writer if he must get it at second-hand. There has been a great pother made since Aristotle concerning the nature of terror, horror, and pity, and their relations to tragedy, and to these erudite discussions reference is hereby made.

The matter of taste is very important, and an author should charge himself with observing it. When pursued to every detail the effect has a peculiar charm. In its fineness it marks the touch of the dramatist. No writer anywhere excels Bronson Howard in this delicacy, and it is the charm of all classic pieces.

The æsthetic part of a play may be its sustaining charm. Verse has a power to carry passages that would be very tedious in prose, just as in opera all action halts until the song exhausts emotion. The eye may likewise be entertained while the mind has small share in the spectacle, as in the ballet, which is almost exclusively an æsthetic thing. The ballet aided by pantomime may be a drama, but the true drama is alone that of the emotions as called forth by action, the drama that leaves an impression of some worthy thing done before us—something for reflection, and not the stuff of a moment's fancy.

3. THE TECHNICAL.—The technique of the drama—the science and art of giving form to

the dramatic material for representation on the stage—does not deal with abstract things like mathematics, and, consequently, is not fixed like mathematics. Certain of its general laws are as steadfast as nature, others are matters of convenience and of experience as to the best results in the use of the existent machinery of the stage. The stage itself is not what it was in the days of Aristotle, and yet he has laid down principles that hold after a lapse of two thousand years.

That part of the technique of the Greek drama that was forced by imagined or real necessities can have no bearing on modern craft. The Greeks gave the performance in a vast auditorium in the presence of a collection of people that would outnumber the aggregate of the audiences on any single night in any of the great cities of this century. Facial expression was impossible beneath the mask. The voice was enlarged by artificial means, the height increased by the sock and buskin. The chorus was a necessity to interpret emotion. The characters were limited. The center gate was reserved for the entrance of certain personages. The recitatives, the fixed law that death should take place behind the scenes, the absence of a curtain to mark the periods, and of any

The Three Elements of a Drama. 41

variety of movable scenery to illustrate; these and various necessities, growing the one out of the other, established for that stage technical laws of its own. It is sufficient to note the facts without setting forth in this place a study of effete things. While morals and æshetics are variable quantities, the means of representation are more changeable still; but all the while there is an advance in this particular, and large freedom of treatment is at hand.

The French with a hard technique of their own had a brilliant period with Racine, Corneille, and their school. The Greeks were imitated, although the form of the French stage and theatre was modern; and the law of the unities was drawn into tense artificiality. It required the genius of Victor Hugo and his associates to disenthrall that stage. The poetical age of Shakspere made blank verse a requirement. This practical century demands prose. Forms of life alter, the forms of the stage must vary. Governments change, the world is always in unrest; and so the large and the small elements of technique are touched. The size of a theatre or the fancy of a manager may create a special technical law. One may confine the scenery to boxed interiors, another may forbid the use of firearms in a play; and so nature and human action may be robbed of their rights. But with the utmost freedom there is limitation always, and within these limitations genius may find its fullest expression. In fact, even where the laws are narrow and vicious, genius has worked with noble patience, and furnished the highest development of some technical principle.

Surely the value of blank verse has been proved by Shakspere, although in losing the art of it we have gained in directness of action.* Whenever a form is once fixed, it has its day and passes into the hands of the imitators, with an occasional true bit of work thereafter, and sometimes a revival of its spirit. In all these forms the real laws are the same; and one of the most hopeful signs of freedom now is that the drama is no longer confined to one or two forms. An account of this emancipation would be a curious chapter in the history of civilization. Lessing had in behalf of Germany a hand-to-hand fight with French methods, and won. We have been in danger of having imposed upon us by the French their views of social morality along with their present perfection of form, and for that reason it is proper that the essential part of

---

* The supremacy of Shakspere in general technique is not in question, but the necessity of cutting the lines of his plays for present stage exigencies is referred to.

morals and æsthetics in technique should be set forth, as well as the right of a theme to its own treatment. With all this freedom of the present period, accuracy is essential.

The first step in technical work is to ascertain the value of the material. It determines whether it is to be used at all. It determines if it is to be done in one act or more.

It is apparent at once that technique is subordinate to the moral and æsthetic elements. The theme dominates in every way. Technical knowledge is impotent if the knowledge of the subject in hand for treatment or the spirit for its use is absent. It is well to emphasize the fact that what is often called technical skill is simply imitativeness and barrenness of the most detestable kind. We see all this illustrated in our Academy exhibitions of painting. Here is an art reducible to mathematical certainties, as, for instance, in linear perspective, and we are asked to admire a man because he can draw a straight line. The skill is so much regarded that we forget to question the value of the idea on the canvas.

The art is cognate with the idea, and cannot be separated from it when the two unite in perfection; but technique is a miserable thing when it does not express worthy ideas.

Here, one artist wastes his paint on a field of vulgar pumpkins, which have the sole merit of suggesting pie.

On the other hand, a master like Jervis McEntee occasionally paints a pumpkin patch with delicacy, but he puts those golden emblems of plenty in that dreamy atmosphere of the ripe year that he alone knows how to establish on canvas. Amid this multitude of painted Venices and outworn subjects done with skill and with authoritative brushes, perhaps, we note the work of some obscure beginner, a simple thing, "The Familiar Path," a lovers' lane in a quiet country nook, leading, in the distance, to the stile on which we used to sit. The title is a happy one, like a whispered word, recalling to us the joys we had in the Arcadia of youth.

It is a true aphorism that one object of art is to conceal art; consequently technique is not addressed to the public. It is a thing of the workshop. That we should feel and say that a play is well done is in the nature of the case; but if it is not well done the public has no further concern with it. The work simply fails. Technique, then, is a matter of course, however much the special observer may analyze and admire it. In some forms of art it may be a material part of the pleasure afforded, but in the drama the illusion and the emotions are far, far more important. It is thus that in fact we forget the author in the actor and the play, and often the poor wretch's name is dropped from the bill.

Just as all forms of the drama—the farce, the opera, the burlesque, the tragedy, and so on—have some distinct technical laws of their own, the themes out of which they grow have natural rights. So powerful is the dramatic idea in this respect, that instinct supplies the rules with such natural artists as Oliver Goldsmith. It is this inherent suggestiveness of the subject that makes perfect dramatists of those youths whose best work is their firstling, as with Sheridan and Boucicault. Preachers, who have no special knowledge of the stage, have written lasting dramas. If technique alone could turn out plays, Boucicault could have long monopolized the market. The English drama has had its being without a written code; although the common law of tradition has been in existence. Let it not be imagined that these laws are not abundant and essential. It is, on the contrary, of great importance that law should govern; but a vital thing that conventionalism do not take the place of that which creates art. The argument of Coquelin, the French actor, is simply a jugglery in terms.

Art does not disdain natural emotion at any step, and the gist of all freedom in work is that a man should express his own thought in his own way, subject to principles. To do a thing in one way simply because some one else did it in that way is a pernicious process. Again, this caution does not trench on the stability and value of law. In acting, beauty will essay expression in one way; the musical voice will largely rest on its notes; and grace will follow the behest of its functions, and has the same right to do so that pure vigor has. Facial expression may be lacking in one, strength in another. By the like urging faculties a dramatist may proceed with the assurance that he is in the highway.

Sheridan's "School for Scandal" is a case in point; and the following analysis is not presented as a new study of the play, but simply to state familiar and possible criticisms, in order to show that an author has the right to follow his own instincts and do his work in his own way, provided he does not depart too far from dramatic lines. Sheridan violated conveniences rather than principles. It is worth while, at any rate, to suggest, in no dogmatic way, a comparison between the rights of genius and the rights of technique as they are involved in Sheridan's drama.

The characters of the play are irregularly defined, but the original cast made living figures of them. They supplemented the work of Sheridan. Mrs. Abingdon gave to Lady Teazle in the scene of the quarrel with Sir Peter the air of a gentlewoman's raillery, while her successors permitted the young wife to resume some of the harshness of voice and inelegance of manner that belonged to the daughter of the country squire. In particular is there need of the actor's art, to make a distinct character of Joseph Surface. In the original draft of the play the author had confused designs as to his use, and even in the matter of naming him cast about with uncertainty, hesitating between half-a-dozen names. Joseph Surface is not sincere even in his duplicity. He has not sufficient warmth of feeling or elegance of manner or plausibility of talk to explain his influence over Lady Teazle, and the incidents of themselves do not justify her confidence or imprudence in visiting his room. But it is a curious feature of the play, as one may discover on close examination, that Sheridan labored to give adequate cause for action as it arose.

Any objection that may be urged against the sequence of the scenes may be found answered in some motive or line, which, however obscure, reveals his purpose. It is an obvious defect, for example, that the two lovers, Maria and Charles Surface, are together in no scene until the last; but Maria has said to her uncle that she obeys him in his command to hold no communication with the profligate. Sheridan's own explanation of it was that he could not trust the two actors to whom the characters were assigned with an interview of the sort. This of course was a confession of weakness rather than a solution.

There are many needless inconsistencies. Sir Peter suspects relations between his wife and Charles, and they are not brought together. The opening scenes promise that Lady Sneerwell will be a factor in separating Charles and Maria, and yet she has little or nothing to do with the action. There is infinite scandal partaken of as at a feast, but none of it, except by reference, is used to bring about the catastrophe, which is effected by the screen. Sir Benjamin Backbite is a lover of Maria, but to no purpose in the action. Mrs. Candour, the most interesting and skillful gossiper of them all, is a perfect figure, without a motive in the play except to kill miscellaneous and outside reputations by innuendo.

But all of this incoherency is overcome by the unflagging interest that is sustained by the glow of wit. A material part of the play is its brilliant repartee and a readiness of wit that simply

The Three Elements of a Drama. 49

destroy all mental differences in the characters as to social position and general purpose. This defect, however, is its merit. The actors who would carry *this* play to its appropriate effects must be skilled in clear enunciation and in the expression of enthusiastic banter. This saving vitality is a kind of action in itself. The play will live because it is the ultimate expression of a phase of society that will exist always, the humors of which will be recognized by each succeeding generation. It can never be supplanted by any new play on the same theme.

Its wit at least is organic. It has four scenes that are perfect in themselves. Lady Teazle will always be the test of genius in acting, and will remain above ordinary capacities. The character must be created every time it is performed. If natural gayety of spirits be lacking in the actress, she will never command the coterie of which the text says she is the most brilliant member. The headlong, heedless rush of the transformed country girl, endangered as much by her innocence as by her vicious surroundings, requires a delicate art. The actress must escape the perils that beset her in the very situations provided by Sheridan, who has not furnished her with the purity that she has a right to make a fight for with her own art.

If the play be lacking in coherent mechanism, it is yet dramatic to a degree rarely seen in comedy. It is a great and effective play in spite of Sheridan's defiance of simple conventionalities. The complex nature of the revelation at the falling of the screen is perhaps unsurpassed in any situation ever devised in comedy. It is true that character is lacking in Lady Teazle, and her extrication, recovery of herself, and her reconciliation to Sir Peter are not sufficiently founded on previous incidents.

The technical construction of "The School for Scandal" is by no means sacred; and, some day, a bold manager, with the courage of common sense, will lay hands on it and remedy some of its "faults"; and yet, after it is done it will be found that the genius of Sheridan was right in certain details that to the modern customs appear to be all wrong. Conventionalism as a substitute for soul is an unmixed evil; while technique freed from imitation in the general and in the particular, except as it is confirmed by principles, is the practical essential of the dramatic art.

It must not be imagined that the comments made on Sheridan's process of work in "The School for Scandal" is a defense of looseness in structure or of ignorance of dramatic canons.

"The Honeymoon," a most successful acting play, may also be cited as containing all manner of violation of rule, but it is an error to believe that genius has no rule. Sheridan knew what effects he wished to produce. The man of genius—or, what is of the same account, the man who freely grasps his subject, general and particular—is conscious of the exact proportions required, and proportion is the secret of power. This fact is familiar to those who read plays submitted to managers. Not half a dozen in a thousand of them show the smallest sense of adjusted relations. Now proportions are tested by the stage performances, and here is where the master of technique can see a step further in advance of even the man of genius. Technique in this relation becomes a practical thing, helpful after the facts of the conception are defined. It comes after the philosophy of the subject has been worked out. Technique alone can never write a great, true, honest play. Perfect knowledge of rule is not everything, for D'Aubignac, the best of the early writers on dramatic art, was a failure as a dramatist. And yet it is supremely absurd to decry scientific sureness in the craft; as much so as to entertain doubt of a writer's ability because he knows the rules of grammar and rhetoric. Ignorance is not necessarily a characteristic of genius. The art can be just as genuine as the nature in a play. The principles of the drama and the structural necessities of it should be entirely familiar to the maker of a drama. Equipped with full information, he does not feel art as a burden at all. He is hardly more conscious of it than is the spectator of his finished product. One reason that the drama is so virile and independent in France is that the art of the stage has there been discussed with fullness and without reserve. Its principles are appreciated by the beginners, and certain conditions, common enough elsewhere, would be laughed at. More than this, theatres like the Français maintain those laws and prove their beauty in exacting obedience to them. Thus the French, living in an atmosphere of the right kind, have a genius for dramatic form as the Greeks had for the sculptured. In a country that inevitably must contribute noble things to the literature of the stage, as it will to other matters of the world's progress, there is need of a thorough understanding of technique. This book may be helpful thereto.

The Frenchman understands the principles of dramatic art as clearly as we do the principles of our political constitution; the essential things of liberty he may know very vaguely.

To knowledge a certain added practical experience is profitable, just as firmness in the musical scales comes from enormous application. Art will never hurt the honest writer. It makes available all material of value. Let a man's genius be backed by it, and he is the one who has the mastery over the human heart above all poets; for what he feels, lives, sees, and dreams comes to us visibly, and our eyes flash at the spoken sentiment, our hearts beat at the noble deed, our eyes moisten at the poetic thing. We see it all done in and for itself, not the author behind it, but nature, God, if you will.

In a poem or a picture you may see the art; in a drama, never; for the action halts wherever a writer spins phrases.

Legouvé says that dramatic technique is as susceptible of improvement as the art of mathematics. This is only true in so far as its principles may be applied to a theme that is grasped in its entirety by a writer. That art only is perfect that allows a freedom that saves the material from conventionalism. Let us glory in Sheridan—not perfect in technique by any means—because he had no meeting between the lovers in "The School for Scandal"! If art were conventionalism, then all dramas would be written alike. The writer may have his method, as he may have his motive. Technique is in general subordinate to the matter, but not at all points. But this has been sufficiently indicated, perhaps.

There is certainly a constant improvement in the practical application of correct principles. The art is forcing itself from old conventionalisms, although it is always in danger of new ones. Let us get at a few examples. It was the custom of writers a decade or so ago to bring all their characters in a circle before the footlights at the end of the last act. This is not false art, but when it is practiced as an eternal law, how absurd! Sardou finishes some of his pieces with two characters. Neither practice is law. The play must have an end,—that is law. The classicists had a rule that the stage could abide no more than fourteen characters. These worthies also thought that conjugal love was not fit for the stage. Corneille denied to love any but a secondary place, and said that it was impossible to represent love at sight on the stage, —surely fatal to our Romeo and Juliet.

Another absurd restriction was that no character should enter upon a given scene more than once. In these and many other rules the student may see reasons and art; but he will gain the conviction that principles and not conventionalities are the factors for an author to work by. The truth is, no art is practiced to its full value if it cannot grapple with the life about us. Imagine the drama restricted, as the early classicists insisted, to Roman or remote history for its themes—one long line of generals, sparse armies, and changeless togas!

In point of fact, there has been a confusion of teaching by reason of basing it all on the fragmentary laws of Aristotle, laws that related almost entirely to tragedy.

CHAPTER III.

THE PRINCIPLE OF UNITY.

UNITY—the absolute and essential relations of all the parts to the whole—is a fundamental rule in all art. The object of art is to produce preconceived effects or results, and every stroke of the workman, be he painter, sculptor, or dramatist, will be impelled by meaning and purpose, and be correct in its detail, in proportion to his sincerity and fullness of knowledge.

He is no artist at all who does not know from the beginning what will come from his hand. The tool must obey the mind; and in the process of creation it uses only those means and those materials that work toward an organic whole. The poet is under exactly the same law that is followed by the maker of a steam-engine, which is designed for the exercise of power; and, surely, that composition of forces—just like the composition of emotions and actions—is effective and even beautiful in proportion to the adjustment of all its parts to this end. In archi-

The Principle of Unity. 57

tecture this rule is visibly the first and last law; for the full effect of the creation is to be gained only when it is viewed at a proper distance to observe the relations of its parts to its entirety. The highest type, the incomparably perfect unity, is the human body, where all is organic.

There is no dramatic unity, then, when the materials are incongruous. The familiar line of Horace that describes false work, to put it into idiomatic English, as "neither fish nor fowl," is the homeliest common sense, and sums up the principle.

The treatment of the subject in the matter of unity is further governed by the law of proportion. Its parts may be congruous but inharmonious, as the bad note in music, the falsely painted line, or even the blotch of color in the painting.

With unity involving the whole work, it is easy to perceive that there must be danger to it at every step, and that there are many forms of unity. The peculiar genius or spirit of an author, for example, furnishes a kind of unity, and so subtle, that incompleted works defy the hand that would bring them to an end. A noted literary torso of this kind is Schiller's drama "Demetrius," that would have been one of his greatest plays had he finished it. The unity of style may be broken by the mixture of comedy and melodrama, and so throughout the list. Indeed, it would seem as if the foundations of comedy writing were breaking up in these times, when so little distinction is made between the elements of comedy and burlesque or farce. Anachronism may break the chain. A reference to the affairs of to-day in a piece laid in some other century, the characters of which would know nothing of this, is a breach of common sense; but a bastard French play written by an American is more reprehensible. Improbability is a mighty factor of failure. Inconsistency of purpose in the persons; discontinuity in the action, by way of episode or otherwise; the introduction of disconcerting argument, or of anything that is false to nature or repugnant to our feelings, or that we cannot accept—all have to reckon with unity. Obscurity in any part is fatal.

Where our sympathy and intelligence do not follow, and where, at the end, the impression is not conclusive after the will of the author, the unity of the piece is at fault. In other words, the technical handling has not brought the material to the fusion point.

Or even take it where the subject and not the treatment fails with the audience, where there is lack of agreement, unity, between author and spectator, it is a like case, for the drama must wholly gain the spectator. This statement belongs to the æsthetic and ethical elements, but it is made here in order to suggest the broad-reaching nature of unity.

If the spectator does not witness a play in its entirety he destroys unity for himself. And thus a critic writing of a first production with imperfect experience of it may inflict a cruel injustice.

Much that has been indicated in this matter is merely by way of suggestion, and awaits enlarged treatment. Nearly all that has been stated is involved in the unity of action, the most important of the traditional three unities upon which we shall now touch.

The French theorists and dramatists sought to establish three unities, thinking to draw them from Aristotle's fragmentary Poetics: 1, the unity of time, which required everything to be done in the assumed space of twenty-four hours; 2, the unity of place, that all should happen on one spot, or within the city walls; 3, that all the incidents should tend to one catastrophe. The attempt to observe these three landmarks governed all the products of the French classic school, and no partisan of an opposed theory can justly deny the brilliancy and power of some of the works of Corneille and Racine. The object of the dogma of these unities was to compel illusion, and illusion is the life of the drama. The theory was sincere, but the arbitrary limits were too narrow. The unities of time and place, as declared by the French, are controverted by an analysis of the Greek plays themselves, and were not, in fact, formulated by Aristotle. They were disproved by Lessing in his *Hamburgische Dramaturgie;* and overturned in the literary revolution in Paris headed by Victor Hugo. They were not observed by Shakspere, that "barbarian," that Voltaire, the Academic, could see no rule in; and they have never had a hold in the English drama. We may suspect them in Ben Jonson; and Shakspere, no doubt, had considered and rejected them.

Finally, these rules, as an inseparable trinity, have been annihilated in a little treatise, a résumé of the whole subject, written by Simpson. This writer goes so far as to say that no play was ever written which held them all without violating common sense.

It would serve no purpose now to go over this discussion, and the very general statement given of the French dogma covers the case.

As to the matter of time, not only in romantic plays, but in the greater number of plays, time is needed for things to happen—happen, that is it—change of character or resolution, based on circumstance, etc. "Camille" has all the unity desirable for the theme, and yet its acts are described in the bill of the play as 1, March; 2, April; 3, August; 4, October; 5, Winter. Within that period a fatal physical disease develops and terminates. In "Eustace Baudin," the child of the first act appears as grown in another. To see the absurdity of a close construction of unity, recall "A Celebrated Case," and note in the meeting between Jean Renaud and Adrienne, advanced to womanhood since they parted, how "unity of time" falls away in that other unity of illusion and full sympathy. For a limited class of subjects the French triune unity is ideally strong and chaste; but it may be noted that verse, as we see in the fine examples of Corneille and Racine, is its essential robe. The limitations of this form of drama press it into such barren action that a purely artificial collocation of speech, melodious, varied, and beautiful in the elocution, must help it out. One necessity of rule leads to another necessity, and the subjects were confined to ancient history, and these great geniuses of the

French drama were mute about their own times; as if there were nothing in any life except that of the dead of other peoples and other days.

This was indeed significant, and could not last. The beauty as well as the evil of declamation, often empty, had to go. Life teems with drama, and under the old rules a vast deal of it could not be touched. It was found that under them material things had to be told that should be acted; that probabilities were sacrificed, absurdities introduced, and nature was twisted in its narrow confines. They were the swaddling garments of the French drama, and it has had undeniable benefit from them. The French writer recognizes the truth that is in them, just as the American citizen recognizes the truth of liberty. There is no discussion here about human rights: there is no doubt in the French mind about the essential value of all these rules. The French writer may have thrown over the absurd argument of Voltaire that if an action of fourteen days is represented all that happens in those fourteen days must be represented. On the contrary, drama is life, and life is made up of infinite detail, and art is the elimination of the non-essential. Things of no concern in any life fall into oblivion, and there is no regret. The unity of action remains imperative. The scope of the action is controlled by the focus into which it may be drawn. The mental and other habits of an audience may have something to do with this. Shakspere's plays, now abridged, were acted in their entirety in their day.

If we regard the intent or the practical bearing of the unities of time, and particularly of place, we see that they are really to a great extent directed against scenery. In a day when the scenic art was not developed, there was high reason for the rules.

And here comes the conclusive proof that the material is greater than the technique in itself—as stated in previous chapters—for its rights swept away the universal force of these rules. Of recent years there has been a reaction against certain evils of scenery, such as the too frequent shifting of scenes. In some theatres a "front scene" is not now permitted, but the subject, as ever, should control, and no arbitrary law is sound, whether made by theorist or stage manager. We are not practicing under the Greek or the French code, nor working under the limitations of the Greek stage, as we are not bound by its morals, or social and religious traditions, or political government. Let us continue to have a wholesome respect for what is true and of value in the triune unity. Sardou adheres pretty closely to the line of all three. The unity of action, or circumstance, including purpose, character, and all that goes to gain the complete sympathy and intelligence of the spectator, remains supreme and inviolable. It is better called <u>the unity of illusion</u>—a term that embraces the three unities.

The uniting of the incidents, or the unity of action, is simply the logic of action. The test is: Do we follow the action along the line of cause and effect? do we accept it? and does it leave an impression that spans the whole performance?

CHAPTER IV.

THE DIVISION INTO ACTS.

THE object of the action of a play is to gain our intelligence, which is followed by sympathy, and this can be done only by a logical sequence of events. The action must have a beginning, a middle, and an end, and these three parts are the natural divisions of a play. The beginning will include a statement of the cause of action; the middle, the development of the action to a crisis; the end, the result of the action. We thus have premise, argument, and conclusion, and these things occur in an action that is brief enough to be compassed in a single act. Custom has divided plays of serious import into five acts, but this is largely a convenience, and there is no arbitrary or magical force in the number. Shakspere's plays were not originally divided into acts. The Greek plays had irregular pauses sustained by the chorus; but Aristotle makes no mention of acts. The division of this chapter into five parts, in treating of the corresponding number of acts, is designed for the convenience of the reader in referring to the many plays so arranged.

The acts are parts of a drama separated by an interval. It is alleged that the spectator supposes certain things to pass in the intervening time. It is not always that appreciable and definite events happen, but the new act begins with an adjustment of conditions as a result of the preceding act. This interval is convenient as a place of bestowal for certain happenings that are material and yet need not be seen. The purpose of action is illusion, conviction, and if after an interval we are told that a certain thing has happened that we know must or should inevitably happen, we believe the statement as it appears in the dramatic development.

It must be a matter of course. It is made a part of the action by the imagination; possibly a scene of unpleasant nature is spared, and space is saved. For example, an act closes with occasion for a duel; the beginning of the following act sees the piece advanced to a point beyond that event. Each act, up to the last act, must have a comparative conclusion, and the last act must be final. Each new act, as said, begins afresh, and usually some new relation or other thing has been formed in the interval. The law, which is purely statutory and conventional—that is to say, for convenience—is meant to provide at the end of an act against incompleteness of the kind described. Thus the curtain cannot fall on a tableau and rise on the same with its unaltered relations.

It would not do to have the duel, as a scene, interrupted by the end of the act, and then resumed, or the missing part of it omitted and described. While modern audiences, unconscious of old rule, do not make much pother about the lapse of time, there are happenings that cannot well stand together in one act. The dear classicists could not have supposed a battle in a play without accommodating the progress of the action to an imaginary lapse of twelve hours. Ponderous incidents had to intervene between expectation and fulfillment. Very well, your battle may go between the acts in the extremity. In modern usage twelve minutes, and not twelve hours, will serve for a very heavy engagement. A character in the play could not well go half-way across the globe and back during the action of an act. He had best make his journey while the curtain is down.

There are practical reasons why there should be periods of rest. There are many plays of great intensity where the chief actor could not by any possibility stand up under the uninterrupted expenditure of energy, physical, mental, and emotional. He would lose in effect at moments requiring the full glow of his power. It is believed by the academicians that the spectator requires the opportunity to gain appreciation of the story in the interval and to enjoy the retrospect; but as audiences are rarely ruminant at such times, we may assume that the true reason or pretext for the interval is partly the imagined necessity or desire for rest. It is easy to note many conveniences afforded by these intervals, and some causes, to be touched upon, natural as well as technical, which may be imperative with certain material; but in the use of other material it is possible that in the evolution of the drama uninterrupted performances will be given without a fall of the curtain until the end of the play. It may then be found that great fire and strength is gained by the swift action, undelayed by the curtain and the pauses. "One hundred francs for you," once said the elder Dumas, "if the curtain is raised before the applause dies away." Instead of three hours, two would suffice to unfold the story, the interest would speed along, the illusion would be deeper, sending the audience home with heightened pulse and warmer enthusiasm. The magic of scene-shifting will be such, after a while, that in the romantic play much will be gained by the continuity. These features are suggested in order to impress the fact that the division into acts is not an integral necessity of every theme. In point of fact, even now, where the facilities exist for quick change of stage, or where the same scene serves for the next act, the interval is not customarily more than a minute or so in duration. When time is imagined to elapse, or something of importance, not acted for some good reason, to occur during an interval, the curtain is indispensable.

In this relation we may dispose of the question of time on the stage. The lapse of time that may be safely left to the imagination depends entirely upon the conditions that make for illusion. We have just seen that the fall of the curtain will provide for any lapse of time, and an author's common sense will teach him not to advance by leaps and bounds in the same act, or, at least, the same scene. The reappearance of a character ten minutes after he has left the stage, announcing that he has been gone half an hour, will be accepted if the action is of diverting interest; but it is not wise to have a clock about, however accommodating it may be.

It is certain that the treatment of the material

is very considerably affected by the division into acts; and these divisions have strong technical reasons for their existence.

Let us add a few to those already stated. These acts present distinct pictures and so assist in the final and full understanding of the play. There is less chance that the general impression be blurred in any of its parts when each act does its work. Scenic necessities have much to do with it also. The conventional division into acts, then, is the point of view from which to proceed in a technical analysis of the structure of a play.

A play is not written in the sense that an essay or a poem is. It is constructed. It is an organism, with connected, articulated parts, that consist of other parts, all with distinct organisms, all co-related, none of which can be taken from the chain without breaking the continuity. Thus a drama is divided into acts, the acts into scenes. They are just as essential to intelligent work as they are to the general understanding of the play in performance. Each scene accomplishes something, and the sum of these scenes makes the act, as the sum of the acts makes the play. These acts cannot be arranged merely with reference to the time of performance or to equality in the number of lines. The mathematical division of an apple is one thing, and the apportionment of effects in a play is another. It is true that Corneille is accurate to a line in some of his plays, but it is a mannerism only. The length of an act is determined by what that act is to accomplish. When it reaches the end of that function the act is done, be it long or short.

The middle of the action—which does not mean a mathematical division into two equal parts—provides the climax, and to this climax the action ascends from the beginning or introduction, and from it falls to the end or catastrophe.

To say that the action rises is plain enough, but to describe it as falling is not entirely satisfactory at first blush.

The interest in a true drama remains to the end. The action declines or falls rather in the sense of direction to an end. The action—without regard to the interest—is narrowed to fewer expedients; the resources of the persons in the strife are fewer; the possibilities of what may happen are narrowed down now almost, or, it may be said, assuredly, to the inevitable. Between the three points of beginning, middle, and end lie the divisions of development and denouement.

Before the beginning of the action (of issue joined), or along with it, there must be an exposition of circumstances; and all these necessities exist in a play of one act or of whatever number of acts. In the three-act drama they would be thus associated: 1, Exposition, or introduction, and beginning (of action); 2, development and climax; 3, denouement and catastrophe or end. In five acts they follow in this order: 1, Introduction and beginning; 2, development; 3, climax; 4, denouement; 5, catastrophe or end. Each of these divisions has its peculiar structure, as remains to be examined. The terms used above in describing the divisions are not better than other terms that may be preferred, such as in the place of development, beginning of the complication; in the place of denouement, untying the knot; introduction for exposition; catastrophe, ending—what you will. Each act is so much a thing for itself that they are all susceptible of descriptive titles, as "Love," "Betrayal," "Death," each of which suggests a play in itself.

The chief concern—the fatal concern—of an inexperienced writer is for a plot. He wants it already prepared in every detail. His anxious inquiry is, "How is a plot made?" as if it were a matter of a few moments. It is not made at all. It is a growth, as has been explained in treating of the theme. Brougham's saying is correct, "A play writes itself." The plot or story is the result of laws in human nature, and no one can codify those laws, modified as human nature is by so many numberless conditions. The plot will be found in the subject and nowhere else; and a plot patched up from various sources is rarely effective. Of course any story, if of dramatic nature, may become the plot of a play, subject to dramatic arrangement and convention; but such things are for the adapters and the "old clo's" men of the profession, who hunt around continually in all manner of literary rag-bags for their stock in trade. Shakspere used many ready-made plots, but he applied to them all the process of germination from the roots.

In one sense a plot *is* made. We arrive at a story by solving a problem. Take the familiar one-act piece in which man and wife at breakfast begin talking with great amiability, become disputatious and quarrelsome, and finally fall again into loving agreement. The object was to present a domestic scene in which the folly of high temper was to be proved. The problem was, how to do it? In other words, you assume a proposition and demonstrate it. It is almost superfluous to say, after what has been said on the value of material, that the proposition must be susceptible of proof.

It is easier for an author to write a play, if he knows how to do it, than it is to steal one. In the same way adaptation may be harder than original work. A play is not a puzzle. Be the theme simple or complex, and it should be neither too simple nor too complex, the play is powerful in proportion to the simplicity of the plot—that is, to its clearness.

Plot is similar to composition in painting. Emotion alone is not plot. Action—with all tending to one point, as in a spider's web—will produce a plot; and in any dramatic theme the main incidents are in plain view to any intelligent author. If we take the biblical account of Samson, we know that a play based on it must include a scene to show the strong man's prowess, another to represent his infatuation for Delilah, and again his imprisoned condition and final pulling down of the temple. We know that jealousy will lead to murder; that rivalry begets suspicion, just or unjust, while other incidents appear to the imagination at once. These are the landmarks, and are to be staked off, just as the surveyor gets his bearings, just as the artist gets his proportions. It is not hard to get a plot if it exists in the subject. The story ought to be susceptible of being told in very few words; and with this simple plot which the author finds or makes, he proceeds to detail. The secret of his work in a nutshell, then, is to so write that, after all is done and told, it is reducible to his original proposition. It is not enough that he never forgets his original design. He must so unfold the story that the audience never forgets what is material for it to know; as, for instance, an individual may be kept in mind and yet be seen rarely or not at all in the action; or, to illustrate by a point of technique, the cause, before stated in the play, may be recalled by a suggestive touch just before the result. In short, a drama should be as plain as a primer. One little omission anywhere, or a fact feebly presented, and forgotten by the audience, may in the end destroy the illusion.

It was once a requirement that there should be an underplot. This was accomplished usually by a love-affair between minor characters. In "Daniel Rochat" it is between Casimir and Lea's sister. In "Camille" it is slight, but integral. It may be required for various reasons, but is not indispensable. It provides padding for plays when the main incident is insufficient or does not of itself furnish sufficient variety.

1. THE INTRODUCTION.—The beginning of a play—the exposition—is in direct relation with the end, and indeed with all that lies between, so that an author who knows exactly the problem that he has in hand lays his foundation with mathematical exactitude. It is here that trained writers like D'Ennery show a beautiful skill, a fine and unlabored touch, that is all the result of absolute mastery of the whole matter before the detail is entered upon. The processes of any particular mind in the evolution of a true play it would be futile to surmise, for the thought of it is voluminous, patient, often perplexed, making a beginning here and renewing the attack there upon a subject; but it is safe to say that the general plot is always well formed in the mind before the introduction is put into shape. It is here that preparation is made for the action and the end. In the introduction are to appear clearly, and as briefly as the subject admits, the conditions out of which the action grows. There is a natural order of facts in every story, and few men go amiss in ordinary talk in relating a personal experience of a dramatic nature. In such a case it is a simple matter of course to state at once the time and place of the happening of interest. "When I was traveling in India, just before the Sepoy

The Division into Acts. 77

Rebellion," or, " During the war, when I was in command of a company under Sheridan in the Valley of Virginia," or, " In the latter part of '49, when I was mining in the Golden Gulch in California," illustrate the simple beginnings of such recitals. All such primary facts must be marshaled in the introduction of a play. These are <u>the antecedents of action</u>. Facts of time, place, and circumstance; facts of color, of tone, of character, and facts of action or plot, press toward expression. Exactly with what force to state them, exactly how much of a fact to withhold, and the form to give them, are matters of judgment and of purpose. When a subject has been thought over and dreamed over until it is ready for the shaping, a quantity of material has been accumulated that must be mastered, for there is more of it than can be used. The preliminary thought—like the studies of a painter—has furnished possibilities, actualities, and touches, that must be sifted; much must be rejected because of superfluity, or because of identity in value or use. It is in the power of will to reject, that one secret of a firm touch lies. Of all this material a part belongs by necessity to the introduction.

There is a great reserve of knowledge in an audience, and it is of importance not to write above or too far below that line of common information. At the present time scenery serves economy in expression, although it may be said, with significance, that it could not supply the magic of the words in the lines of Shakspere's "As You Like It." Costume tells its own story also. General character is visible in the actor's counterfeit, as is his station in life and probable use in the story. Local color and the place of action are given in the painted cloths. These let us call passive facts. They at least confirm the text, and give, at once, needful *general* impressions.

Let us illustrate for a moment how D'Ennery in "The Two Orphans" proceeds from the general to the particular. It is a good example, too, of a play springing into instant life. The curtain rises and we see the Pont Neuf, by the river Seine, a familiar mark in the heart of Paris that we know; the city lying before us; picturesque types of people, and the whole scene full of color; all with a general purpose. This is the city of beggars and rascals and libertines, of wealth and of poverty.

Note the immediate juxtaposition of La Frochard and the Marquis de Presles. We first, and on sight, know Frochard as a beggar only. Five lines, and she is off, not to reappear for a considerable space. The Marquis unfolds his own character in telling of the vision of a beautiful girl in a chaise, seen while returning to Paris. His valet had been conferred with. There is villainy in hand. The Marquis speaks incidentally of the sister of this vision. He tells his friends to come to Bell Air that evening. The two travelers, the girls, are to be met by a relative, an old citizen. He is spirited away by the valet. Then in scenes are exhibited the true character of La Frochard, and the relations of Jacques and Pierre. And so the story runs with absolute clearness, each scene definite and impressive. Always does D'Ennery first suggest and then confirm. It is not until the tenth page of the printed play that we learn that Louise is blind. The helplessness of the two sisters, the certainty of disaster to them, was enough at first; then the withheld fact—the blindness—comes with a thrill. D'Ennery introduces facts of person, of character, and of plot with masterly effect and order, and expresses the relations between people at exactly the right time.

So much for the present, by way of indicating the process of coming from the general to the particular. All the causes and motives of future action lie in the introduction. It contains all the possibilities. In "The Two Orphans" it is the rescue of Marianne from suicide by Henriette—a mere incident in point of time in acting—that leads to the climax of the powerful third act; and there is hardly a scene or a saying that does not cross some thread in the woof. All is prepared for, and nothing is sudden, for in this introduction the Doctor examines Louise's eyes, and the hope of restoration in the last is not a mere device. The scene of conflict between Pierre and Jacques is squarely founded on scenes in the first act, and in the proof then proffered that the Frochards " come of a family that kill." It has been said that action precedes character in importance, but a fact of character may be identical with a fact of action. It is better to suggest rather than to dwell on chance in the introduction.

This introduction contains the promise that must have fulfillment. Emphasis must be made on the points that are to be moving forces. The sympathies are to be directed, but if action is to grow on the line of sympathy, it is obvious that an introductory scene involving it must not be exhaustive. The wishes and purposes of the characters are to appear, and at a certain point of complexity in this first act the clash of opposing interests is sure to come; with it come curiosity and interest, and the function of the first act is thus completed.

The Division into Acts.

The action must unfold itself out of the present feelings and relations of the actors. It is not the less certain that in order to bring the action into the desired limits or a certain focus, that antecedent happenings of, perhaps, years before, must be stated. If the exposition of such facts be not made a part of the action, the statement had as well, if not better, be printed in the program or spoken in a prologue; for the facts become truly effective only when treated in the technical way. When they are told as a mere artifice, directed to the audience and not to a person of the drama, action halts. It is exactly at these points that technique becomes of supreme importance to the author. He has his material. How is he going to contrive to get certain facts into evidence? There are many ways, good and bad. It requires a nice judgment and a patient mind to determine between them. The author must make the occasion—be it a confidence between lovers; a quarrel of recrimination in which facts familiar to the two are brought out; or a soliloquy, etc. There is no excuse for clumsiness in these elementary things.

Action should be like the arrow sped from the string.

Othello tells of his antecedents and of his courtship of Desdemona in a situation of dramatic intensity before the ducal court of Venice.

His words are not addressed to the audience in a theatre. The Ghost of Hamlet's Father gives a bit of unrevealed history in a form that is surely dramatic.

The rehearsal of a story obviously intended for the audience alone is clumsy, and begets doubt in the skill of the author. However, a long recital seems necessary at times. Daniel Rochat's account of himself to Bidache is an example.

To be dramatic, the mechanical object must be concealed, and there should be reason for the hearing as well as for the telling.

Note how that is managed throughout the scene in "Caste." Hawtree says: "Tell us about it—you know I've been away," etc. In "Eustace Baudin," to a new-comer it is said: "You are our neighbor and should hear our little history." Note that the figure is practically created for this purpose—as a medium of information, and for a scene at the close. An unskillful writer would have permitted Baudin and wife to go over the story between themselves, in order to give it to the audience. Narrative is entirely proper used in the right way. Note in "Marble Heart," Marco's passionate recital of her history. The occasion for narrative we usually find in the introduction, but it may occur later on, where it is more readily handled, as in the case just cited. Proper use of narrative may be seen in " Under the Gaslight," where Pearl tells Ray about Laura's early history.

The confidence and pleasure of the spectator should be gained in the beginning. He is a perverse and unworthy hearer, indeed, if he be not then in a receptive state. He submits himself entirely to you. He may combat you later on if your preparation for the gist of the drama is inadequate.

Clearness is an essential and fundamental rule —its quality being more telling than in rhetoric itself. Preparation is the solvent. It has infinitely to do with clearness. Note in Sardou's "Scrap of Paper " (" Pattes de Mouche ") how our attention is called to the statuette of Flora by the warning of the housekeeper to the servant not to touch it. It is not required that we suspect the use to which it is to be put. The dramatist makes the technical point and passes on. Ten pages farther the two former lovers speak of the statuette, and then we see what quaint and wonderful relations it has with the action. Thus the action proceeds without a jolt or a pause. It is established in our belief step by step that a love-letter was left in this Love's post-box three years before by the woman since married, and that it is there now. Imagine this preparation lacking, and Louise explaining for the first time at this point, to Prosper Couramont and the audience, that the room has not been opened for three years. Imagine Marianne, in the third act of "The Two Orphans," suddenly, and without the motive afforded by the incident in Act I., offering herself for transportation in the place of Henriette. Preparation and motive are both in the account here. In this way motives and situations are explained by antecedent facts, and not by a present explanation by the actor of his feelings. It at any rate leaves perfect freedom in the handling of such text.

The spectator is part author of a play. By his interest, curiosity, and anticipation he builds like the author. Everything must be made clear to his understanding, for to it the emotions are subordinate. Clearness does not require that the special use of the statuette, Flora, be stated, or even suggested at once. There is a nicety of art in revealing facts that is governed by the material. There are *coups de théâtre*, such as disguises suddenly thrown off, as of Sir Thomas Clifford in "The Hunchback," but these are surprises that are cleared up in a flash. All that has gone before affords instant explanation. It is not the unexpected that always happens in the drama. It is a question of occupying the mind and the sympathies by way of illusion, and thus it is possible, paradoxical as it seems, to maintain interest and curiosity in a play that we have seen a hundred times. It requires, perhaps, all the more skill for that reason. It is obligatory not to reveal too much, so as not to take away the interest.

Clearness in the evolution of an action does not always require an immediate statement of a fact. When and how to state a fact are conditional. An audience has satisfaction in divining, and are willing to await recital. There is always some impression or effect that is of the first importance. We see this in the case of Adrienne in the beginning of the second act of "A Celebrated Case." The suggestion that this is the daughter of Jean Renaud is of the faintest kind. It is hardly in the text, but it is enough. It is indeed the present, and not the past, that most concerns the story at this point. Soon the story begins anew with the force of the first happenings an active part of it. On the other hand, at the opening of an act the story cannot proceed without a mass of facts plainly stated. As the first instance at hand, examine Act II. of "Eustace Baudin."

That there must be skill in selecting the time and manner of stating facts, implies that they must not be given in bulk or in a jumble. What is to be stated and what is to be acted, and when, is a matter of weighing effects; and is peculiarly technical, for the technical concerns effects. The author must stand back from his work from time to time and regard it as a spectator; and he will often find technical necessities that are absolutely pitiless. And yet technique is generous. The manner of bringing forward these facts it leaves to the touch of the artist, and in the nature of the human mind it could in no two cases be identical, though the effect might be substantially the same, if two dramas were written by two authors of equal skill on agreed facts. In " A Scrap of Paper " the fact that Anatole and Mathilde are lovers could for the moment have been announced by the servants in their conversation, but these lovers are important, and about the first business of the action is to prove this fact, not suggest it merely, and to get them out of the way by means of a scene that makes certain promises of action up to which they must live. You know what to expect of them. They are definite. When the point of condensation, definiteness, is reached, author and spectator alike are at ease in the progressive development. In "The Silver King" the murder must be acted.

There are some facts that unmistakably belong to the gist of the matter. They must be given a place in the acted evidence. In any play concerning William Tell, his marksmanship must be shown early in the action. Accordingly, both Schiller and Sheridan Knowles impress at the very opening of the play the skill of the hunter. In "The Courier of Lyons" the first scenes possess us with an absolute acted comparison of Lesurques and Dubosc. Description would not answer.

While the unexpressed, the indefinite, and the unexplained will leave an effect ineffective, on the other hand over-fullness and elaboration may weary, and so blur impressions. The fact should be so put that it will be recalled instantly, for the spectator must always be up with the action. In the prologue of "A Celebrated Case" an important point is the hot temper and jealousy of Jean Renaud. He becomes an innocent convict mainly on that point. We see nothing but love for his wife in the action; but the conditions under which this hot temper and jealousy are referred to make the impression.

It would be misleading to set up a rule that we find in the jargon of technique, that the action of the introduction must be quiet. In the nature of the case it usually is. It must certainly be a clear dramatic statement of facts, but, among such fine examples as Shakspere furnishes, we can hardly say that it is a quiet action where Iago and his companions at midnight hammer at Brabantio's door, or in "Romeo and Juliet," where it opens with a street-brawl. To say that the action should not be at its height in the introduction is one thing, and to deny animation to it is another. The anger of Brabantio at the elopement of Desdemona really does not touch the issue of Othello's jealousy except in the way of prophecy, and so is merely incidental. There are no proportions in the play disturbed by it.

A "quiet beginning" to a play has a certain value—and is in the nature of nearly all plays—because a number of general impressions are to be conveyed at once; and a point of special significance should not be lost in the state of unreadiness in which an audience often finds itself; but to "give an audience time to settle" is not necessarily a rule.

Care should be taken that the beginning is not on too high a note. This is a correct principle, but this book of technique shall not draw

The Division into Acts.

the false law out of this principle that a play shall not open with masses. It depends. An immobile tableau is certainly faulty.

Everything in a play may be regarded as a fact, and facts as values, as the painters say; consequently sympathy is not to be evoked too strongly at this stage, any more than any other part of the order of facts and emotion is to be anticipated.

The introduction should be careful and contain all the essential facts, but disproportionate length is to be guarded against. The material is usually at fault where overmuch exposition is required. What and how much to give in this introduction is determined by the material only. The first act must be perfect in itself as a part of a whole. It must accomplish something, and be a completed standpoint from which the development of the action may be considered. It must embrace continuity and preparation. In "The Two Orphans" there is introductory matter in all the first three acts, but each act takes you a literary league onward.

The style of the play and tone of the action are indicated in the introduction, so that a farce does not begin like a melodrama. From the overture we divine the tempo of a piece, the passion and the pace with which it is to progress. In none of its elements should the notes be struck too high.

While there is movement from the very beginning of the first act, it is when issue is joined that the action really begins. The clash of interests arrives and the first propulsion is felt. It is the immediate cause of action that follows the unfolding of the general causes. The moment the hero of the play, or his following, or the opposing force, announces a purpose, the mechanism is set in motion. In " Richard III." it begins at once. In " Julius Cæsar " the propelling force is the thought to slay Cæsar, which takes expressive form among the conspirators when their design to slay Cæsar becomes clear. It must occur in every first act, and is usually not distant from the conclusion of it. It should not be elaborated to the impairment of what is to come.

The tendency of the introduction is to clear the decks for action after the clash. There is no part of Shakspere's technique that is more obvious than his plan of bringing forward his personages in the first act. There can be no absolute rule about the introduction of people; but the sooner the formalities are over the better. Sometimes a character exists as truly in the intervening acts as it may in the third, although its appearance may be delayed until then, as Meg Merrilies in "Guy Mannering." It may exist in the spectator's reserve of knowledge, as Queen Elizabeth in Schiller's play, or the character may not appear at all. The material determines even in this important part of technique.

The ancient prologue is a form of introduction to a play that has fallen into disuse. Father Time no longer comes on and imparts necessary information.* There are also acted prologues that are not organic parts of the immediate action. They are one-act plays in themselves, but the beginning of larger stories. Usually they present a different period of life, as the schooldays of Jane Eyre, while the drama is of Jane Eyre's womanhood. The tone and quality of the prologue may differ from that of the drama and may suffer in various disadvantages of not being altogether organic with the main play. The prologue is often essential. It is so in "Monte Christo." That hero of melodrama could not with effect merely tell of his imprisonment and escape.

A story is romantic rather than dramatic, if it requires elaborate preliminary statement—as distinguished from preliminary action. Preliminary

* See "Winter's Tale," etc.

action may in the necessity of the case at times be tedious.

Where there are many things not in the action proper, but to be understood, it is awkward. Material taken from everyday life, with the conditions known to everybody, is favorable to virility. Hundreds of little things need not be stated then; and the author is apt to at once strike into a vital action.

The recital of particular facts must be made by the right people and not by the mechanical process. The housekeeper in "A Scrap of Paper" warns the servants not to touch the statuette on the mantel, "because, etc." The audience could have been apprised of the same facts by the two domestics, but the Sardou touch in this instance is fine and correct.

The problem of the play must appear very soon by a suggestion. Outlines may be foreshadowed, although it is crude practically to announce the entire story. A certain distance ahead the audience may see or think they see.

If there is any doubt about the acceptance of the main issue in a play the introduction should be conciliatory. It should always be agreeable.

The French classicists used to say that the action should begin on "an important day," the eve of battle, and the like; all of which applies to tragedy and sounds like the jargon of conventionalism. It is a specimen of how "laws" are made to serve in the place of principle. In the nature of the case in a drama, the beginning is not very remote from the clash, and the climax is soon in view, but the "important" day or the impending battle may well be lacking.

There are bits of conventionalism that an author need not be afraid of. No one hesitates to use a word because other people use it, and it amounts to the same thing. The chambermaid with the feather duster is of legitimate stock.

Old devices of this minor sort, if they excite ridicule from age, may for the moment interfere with illusion, and, it is true, illusion should begin at once. The old trick of two characters drawing their chairs together and under some pretext of conversation relating to the audience preliminary facts, is bad and always has been. In the right way the two characters seated may begin true action by talk.

Conventional beginnings, perfectly proper in themselves—now outworn—used to be a chorus of villagers or of huntsmen with "Hark to the sound of the stirring horn," or "List to the bugle," etc.

Expectation, suspense, satisfaction—are the

three parts of a play. If the <u>first act excites interest and curiosity as to what is to come, its work is done</u>. The curiosity should not be of the kind that does not allow full attention to the scene immediately in hand. It should end with something <u>definite accomplished, and should establish the first experience of suspense</u>.

It will be observed that much more is said about the first act than the others. This is because principles applicable to the whole are there encountered; and they are treated by way of convenience at once, even though they are to be discussed in other relations.

2. THE DEVELOPMENT.—The second act of a play of five acts is devoted to the development of the action, bringing it one stage forward to the climax, the end of the third act. This is purely convenience. We must not forget that the division into acts is accidental and not organic. Whether a play be in one act or more, its natural parts are, the introduction and clash, the development and climax, the denouement and end—expectation, suspense, satisfaction. The clash comes invariably in the first act, if act there be. The development may make the second act in the order of the five. It is really a division of the matter that lies between the

clash or the issue joined and the climax. The matter may or may not be ample for this use of it. The movement of the play now has a definite trend. It often happens that new characters must be awaited in this act, but the issue is quickly made, and the problem is to advance the action to a given point. In "Daniel Rochat" the first act closes with the engagement of Lea and Daniel.

The issue is joined then. The danger to the union is surmised. The second act, or the development, carries the action to the civil marriage, which prepares for the climax at the end of the third, where there is a split, which appears almost irreconcilable, over the religious ceremony. In "The Danicheffs," a play in three acts, we have development and climax in the second act. Act I., introduction and clash, where the mother, the countess, has the serf girl, beloved by her son, married to another serf; Act II., in which the attempt is made to interest the son in St. Petersburg society, and after certain incidents he learns of the treachery of his mother, reproaches her in a powerful scene, a climax, and leaves to search for Anna. "The Courier of Lyons" illustrates the same thing: Act I., introduction and the clash, where the father mistakes Dubosc for his son, Joseph

Lesurques; Act II., development and climax, where the examination by the magistrate seems to prove the guilt of Lesurques. It so happens that the material does not require the making of two acts out of the second act. In other pieces it is in the nature of the material that development and crisis should be distinct. In "The Lady of Lyons" we have the introduction and the conspiracy to marry Pauline, then the marriage as Act II., and then the climax of Act III. in Pauline's discovery of the deceit practiced on her. When development forms a second act it is because of the value of its closing scene; because it is a natural point of interval; because its ending promises a climax. Its contents depend on the object or nature of the play, for the action of a drama may be rapid or slow, or it may require development of character rather than of plot. There is no fixed proportion of elements in a play. It may be added that any act of a play has its beginning, its middle, and its end, very much as has the play, considered as a whole. Interest in a drama is to be made cumulative, and the second act in its detail and entirety must serve that end.

The scenes, gathering force, and full of meaning, now form situations.

The nature of situation may be pretty well illustrated by reference to a play called "Fate," the genius of whose author enabled him to get his situations by main force if he could not get them in any other way. In "Fate," an adventuress has somehow—no man can explain exactly how—installed herself in the house of a wealthy gentleman. By a series of mistakes and absurdities she separates man and wife. The husband of the adventuress, early in the action, while her plot is forming, suddenly and unexpectedly enters the room where she is. She is standing before a large glass and sees his face reflected there. Her danger is great, for the husband is desperate. In a loud voice he tells how she had abandoned him, of his despair and poverty. He is a tramp; she in silks. How to get rid of him? She is about to be exposed and the victory is apparently his. Suddenly she turns on him and reminds him that he has escaped from a lunatic asylum. So it goes.

A situation must touch the emotions. A mere arrangement of unprepared and unexplained material for situations is of no value. Sheridan makes it very ridiculous in "The Critic," when Puff says, "There's a situation for you! there's a heroic group! You see the ladies can't stab Whiskerandos—he durst not strike them for fear of their uncles—the uncles durst not kill him because of their nieces—I have them all at a deadlock! for every one of them is afraid to let go first."

A situation is never reached without preparation. That preparation may be brief, as in "Gisippus," where the action begins almost at once in the appearance of an old lover on the day of marriage.

There are certain elements in a play that are stronger in one act than in another, but the dramatic idea appertains to every scene in the action, so that curiosity is not excluded from the remaining acts because it is the first function of the first act, and so on reciprocally. Curiosity is one of the begetters of interest, and with the second act begins the task of sustaining the expectation already excited. The object of the first was to get, the second to keep, the attention.

Interest, of course, must exist everywhere. The author must keep it at all hazards. If he finds that attention flags, he may suspect his theme, or, likely enough, its treatment. Genuine device may help him out. Change of scene or idea may be needed. Interest is that which excites curiosity, sustains attention, and produces sympathy. Nothing but action can hold the interest for an entire evening. Interest is stimulated by the situations; and those situations must cohere with character and purpose. Uncertainty is its chief promoter. Episodic interest is not enough. A situation is the state of persons in the scene with regard to others. In a sense all scenes are situations, but the technical meaning is confined to points of special interest, where expectation is peculiarly alert as to what the characters will say and do.

Several persons are thrown into emotion. We realize from the preceding scenes the possibilities. We ask, what will be the outcome? It is a moment of contradictory sentiments in the characters, of suspense in the spectator. We see a figure who must decide between love and honor; patriotism and domestic ties; and so on. There is doubt. There are as many elements of emotion possible as life may afford.

Interest leads to suspense. Suspense as to the issue should remain in the mind; suspense as to a particular situation is a multiple of it. Some plays are carried forward almost entirely by suspense. "Jim the Penman" is of this character. "Diplomacy" is another example. The result is suspended to the last. In situations relations are changed, but you see no ending.

In this, the second act, begin to appear the devices of retardation and delay—the art of suggesting and withholding gives life to the story; expectation has set in, and now it is newly nourished. In "Jim the Penman" the action returns upon itself in constantly new complications. If the action of a play were direct, it would soon come to an end. Here the complication in the action begins. It may be an unexpected event. A situation, in short, is brought about. It excites a state of affairs that must be settled. In real life we would say, "Something has to be done about this." To such resolutions we are constrained by some opposing force, personal or social.

3. The second division of a play, with a beginning, middle, and end—to which, for convenience, may be assigned the third act in a five-act play—contains the gist of the purpose, the complexities, and the peril. The conflict has developed into a story and definite situation. The figure of chief interest must here reach an apparently decisive moment, and the problem that our heart or our curiosity concerns itself about is now to be almost apparently solved, except that possibilities remain to be told in the future action. The ominous moment has hastened its steps, and we are approaching the

crisis or the climax of the story. It can after this go no farther on that line and upward. It must change its source. It is the most important scene, and requires careful elaboration to sustain the quality of the real climax—its ending. It is not necessarily the scene of the greatest sympathy, for the catastrophe may have to stir up depths of emotion, or, in the matter of humor, the denouement may demand livelier tribute. In fact, in tragedy for example, there is here a chance for the hero; in the end, or the catastrophe, there is none. The climax is intense generally, and important always, and appears for the moment to be decisive. In plays of three acts the climax is at the end of the second, as in "The Courier of Lyons," where Joseph Lesurques is pronounced guilty by the magistrate; as in "Article 47," where Cora, by her well-guarded threats, gains the deadly mastery of George Duhamel; as in "The Danicheffs," where Count Vladimir, learning of his mother's treachery in forcing the marriage of the serf that he loves to Osip, renounces the present splendor of the Court, and goes to seek the girl; as in "Caste," where the Marquise visits Esther Eccles, learns of her son's marriage to her, and appears to triumph, in her war of caste, in the departure of her son to the distant and perilous campaign of the soldier; as in "A Scrap of Paper," where the half-burned note is thrown out of the window, after all the busy intrigue, only to renew the danger. In the five-act play, the third act is the natural point for the climax, followed by the even more intense crisis of the fourth act. In " Daniel Rochat " it is the scene in which the freethinker's relentless determination of character is confronted by the religious principles of the woman who is already his wife by the civil ceremony. They finally go apart on this, but not before their resolution is tried by passion and temptation. In "Camille" the climax—or we may call it the height of the action—comes with the interview between the woman and the father of her lover, followed by her struggle of emotion in the severance, and her departure, her sacrifice of self. From these few cases alone it is sufficiently manifest that the climax is begotten of action, compounded of it through and through. It cannot exist without a plot; being the middle of a beginning and an end does not alone bring it about. If it is not compounded of all that has gone before, it is no climax, it matters not how thrilling it may be in itself—a scene of shipwreck or a murder. The jackals among playwrights are constantly appropriating material that in place works with power, out of place, by its feeble effect, protests the user a mere thief. Anti-climax is a term general in its application, and it may occur at any point where lesser interest follows a greater.

The climax is a growth toward the strong finality of the scene of the most intense importance in the play. If there is an irregularity in the growth, whereby a more powerful moment, one stronger in decisive quality, intervenes before the strong close of the scene, there arises an anti-climax. It must be noted that muscular action or other mere animation does not make the preceding moment the more powerful. Sardou and Dumas have taught the wholesome lesson that a climax does not necessarily require explosive material. Observe the quiet climax of "Daniel Rochat."

The climax of a play is a turning-point. Whether or not it shall be a thrilling situation depends upon the material. In melodramas the climax is worked up to with great solicitude; character is added to character, and so on.

Again, the climax of a play is simply its most important situation. It is marked by suspense and quickened expectation, sympathy and expectation leaping out to meet the acted event like an electric spark. The situation being prepared for, the question is how to hold the suspense. The scene cannot last long, and is often explosive in its suddenness. In either event it is effective in proportion to the preparation. It is the point to which all has tended, as the duel in "The Corsican Brothers." In this case the situation is long foreseen. In "Under the Gaslight" there could not be any anticipation of such an incident as the tying of Sharky by Byke to the track of the railroad and his rescue by Laura; but it is all probable in its dramatic relations. In the scene itself the work of detail and preparation is admirably done. In order to have suspense there must be doubt and danger. It is a culmination of all the causes of suspense. A strong situation of suspense is in the last act of "Damon and Pythias," where Damon is awaited by Pythias on the scaffold; and the suspense is held as the time is noted before the execution—six minutes left—then two—and then one! In the final scene in "The Lady of Lyons," the climax of the act, the crisis of the play, we see a conflict of emotion and suspense in the incidents of the hurried action. We are told that Pauline is to marry Beausant; then her own feeling in the matter is revealed; then we see that the sacrifice is needed to save her father, etc. We note reason in every step.

There must be expressed cause for retardation, and proof must be given of every motive.

The climax being a crisis, or moment of doubt, it is not entirely satisfactory in a book of technique to fix it after the arbitrary models of custom. There may be many critical moments of doubt. There is no exact middle of a play, but the climax is at the end of the beginning and at the beginning of the end, wherever that point may be.

4. The denouement follows. The way and the resources for clearing up the action are prepared here. The second and third acts were filled with obstacles; the solution now begins.

Again it may be repeated that the end of the play—its third division—includes the denouement and all that lies between it and the catastrophe. This arrangement of a fourth partition or act is a convenience in the production of effects, and is here used as a convenience in the discussion of construction. Everything in the action heretofore has led up to the climax, to the supreme crisis of the drama, leaving yet room, perhaps, for other effort. The person or persons of commanding interest have been placed in a position of peril—and peril is the proper term, sufficiently descriptive in comedy as in pieces of more serious import—and we must now restore them to their first interest or dash their hopes to the logical ending of the action. The conditions of the plot are about to be fulfilled.

In bringing about the end there must be no lack of vigor, of intensity, of interest, of suspense. If it be done too suddenly, the vitality goes. It is possible for an author to mistake the real crisis of his material. We may imagine a writer, inappreciative of the possibilities that lie in "Daniel Rochat," completing his action with what is with Sardou his climax at the end of the third act. The two lovers practically separate at that point on the issue of civil or religious marriage. In point of fact the strongest scene is in the act of denouement, the fourth. Daniel visits the apartment of Leah at night, and Leah's struggle of passion and the meditation that comes after it clearly lead away from the consummation of marriage. There is, of course, always doubt about her resolution, but an unseen fact has been established with all the intensity and interest of this act; it is a preparation for the end. Up to the climax and its crisis, all tended toward the union, afterwards all worked for the separation. If love held its way strenuously at first, so it existed in the denouement, but the new element of doubt and the means of dissolution overcame it.

Certainly no new facts and fresh devices that are not referable to the past action enter into this part of the play. New characters may be required, but their scope of action is narrower. There is a touch of finality about them all. In the beginning promise of character and action marked every step; here, while expectation is an element the horizon closes down. Change of relative position so distinguished in the progress up to the climax proceeds, but on other lines. When Lady Macbeth walks in her sleep and reveals her madness we know that the springs of action in the play, at least from this side, are available no more. One by one the hopes of Macbeth, based on prophecy, are destroyed. Strong effects, elevation of the scenes, striking situations, emotion, animation— all things that enter into the vigor of a play have room here, but they must count for solution. Retardation was a charm of the upward action; it is now a charm of the downward. The unskilled author is tempted at this point and later on to substitute explanation and description for action; but progressive movement is as essential here as anywhere. Large effects and large traits are required.

In some plays that are constructed with apparent precision of technique the interest ceases before the end. This is the case with "A Parisian Romance." By an accident of good acting, Baron Chevrial, the *roué*, a remarkable study of character, engages the entire attention, and we care little or nothing for the return home of the erring and repentant wife of another figure in the play. This " defect defective " is not in this or in any other case always past cure, but it is for author, actor, and manager to determine if they and the public wish to sacrifice proportion to certain effects. In this particular case it was the genius of Richard Mansfield that was superior to the play.

The end of the scene or act of denouement is always some fact that promises the catastrophe. In the third and last act of "The Courier of Lyons" this point of the denouement is where Jeanne, the outraged and abandoned wife of Dubosc, determines to save Lesurques by revealing the hiding-place of Dubosc. She speaks with Daubenton, the magistrate:

> *Jeanne.* But I will save him or avenge him.
> *Daubenton.* Do you know where Dubosc is?
> *Jeanne.* Follow me!

Somewhere between the beginning of the denouement and the catastrophe there is often a moment of reaction—not merely of suspense, but of heightened hope; such as an attempted or suggested rescue or escape, as in "The Two Orphans"; but this may be reckoned as a device under the general rule of retardation of the action.

5. The catastrophe, or, to use a less technical term, the conclusion, is effected by the gradual process of the last act, or by that part of a play, divided or undivided, that corresponds to it.

This conclusion can never be a mere artificiality. It is the logical result of all that has preceded it. It is organic and must be final. It is an end of the action, or it is nothing. Every question suggested by the play is answered rightly in it as to the past and the possible future of the persons in it. The deeper the emotion aroused by the actor, the more important the subject, the more interesting the plot, the more definite, if any qualification is at all possible, will be the result, the impression, or the conviction of mind. To deviate from the logical result is to destroy at one blow all unity, to extinguish at one breath the vital spark of all. To map out a new life or to suggest a new story on new lines is woful waste. Bad art and false sentimentality are poor counselors.

The question of treatment is very important here. The author is no longer in doubt. His work is over except to impress the ending. Words must needs be few, and yet he must not be too abrupt. Controversy is over, and the author's heart and mind and skill are called upon to give the touch of farewell before committing this emotion in its entirety to the people.

The catastrophe should not be a surprise, just as it should not be abrupt. There is a preparation in every movement of the drama. The more powerful the impression, let us say by way of illustration, of a tragic fate, the more distinctly should its shadow fall backward in the action. Note how Shakspere in "Julius Cæsar," in something like a pause in the action, in a most beautiful episode, has the ghost of Cæsar appear to Brutus, in the solitude of his tent at midnight, before the battle of Philippi. In "Richard III." it is the same token of the certain future. Romeo kills Paris before Juliet's tomb that we may feel the pitiless end that approaches.

The happenings here should be organic. Accident is no part of thoroughly dramatic material. It is a refuge and a device. It cannot be outlawed, for it sometimes serves a purpose, as when the accidental discharge of a pistol slays the villain, or the rich uncle comes

The Division into Acts.

home from India in the nick of time, or, as in "The Rent Day," when the saving cash drops out of the back of a chair that is broken.

In the cases cited there may be a connection with the action, slight but sufficient. The question of probability has most to do with the dramatic value of accident. It is always suspicious and generally faulty.

A play is really ended the moment interest and curiosity cease. As long as they hold, the author keeps his mastery. It is a bad denouement when long speeches are necessary to tell the persons of the play of happenings that the spectators already know of. The actors should be in a position not to inconvenience the audience.

The end of a play is always a change of condition for the principal personages—it is from trouble to tranquillity; from unhappiness to happiness, and the like contrasts. It is final.

The end must not be too sudden. It is subject, and with particular force, to the general law of gradation of effect. It must be in proportion with cause and effect. It must afford a commanding point where the whole action may be recalled. The idea must dominate here as in a musical composition. It must come to a full stop. All doubts must disappear. An earthquake in itself and by itself could not rightly end a play. The end must be organic.

CHAPTER V.

THE SCENES AND PRINCIPLES OF ACTION.

SCENES are of two kinds: (1) the painted picture; (2) what takes place.

As already set forth, each act has its special function, and has a distinctness and a relative completeness of its own. An act is made up of scenes, just as the play is made up of the acts, and these scenes have a similar significance and definiteness of their own; but in the sequence of the onward movement they admit of no pause. If it be taken as an illustration and not altogether as a law, the closeness of the parts may be represented thus: First act; second act; third act: fourth act; fifth act. That is to say, semicolon, colon, and full stop, with the comma between the scenes. The play, the acts, the scenes, are built up by a succession of significant movements and motives and bits of expression, and all, to the smallest particle, must have definite purpose. All scenes are incidents leading up to a main incident. It is astonishing how small a touch, how momentary a flash of character, or what not, may have a value that is to be measured by its quality alone; and, again, time may be required for the impression.

To begin, then, with a broad statement: a scene is not a scene unless it accomplishes something toward the general result. The impression made by a scene may be very strong of itself, very beautiful, very pathetic, very comical, but if it does not belong in every fiber to the action, dramatic law has no pardon for it. It must, moreover, be in its sequence; so that the mere division of an act into scenes is of no more avail than the mere division of a play into acts. It also follows that the length of a scene is determined by its purpose and effect. An act may be composed of one scene or a dozen scenes. They are the dramatic mosaics that enter into the picture, the portions out of which the poet hammers together his action. This distinctness sometimes enables a writer to begin his composition with one of these completed parts. His fire may be kindled at such a point. It is by these steps that he proceeds, through these dramatic movements that his spirit works. This does not imply that a play may not be built in the order of its final shape, but it does mean that dramatic authorship is construction and not offhand writing.

The dramatist is first sure of his general play and of what is needed for each act. The true author's imagination is not restricted by the stage in his formative meditations, meditations that create the play; but when he arrives at the scenes it is a question of detail, and with a firm touch he can work out each scene, can rest, deliberate, choose, reject, and determine length and value with precision. It is here that a secret pleasure is his portion, for the play takes on its true proportions. It begins to breathe. The scene under the author's hand assumes a function known only to him, and in the performance will have its best effect when it again visits the spectator's quick and sympathetic memory some stages on. The author feels the power of his machinery. With every stroke he makes an impression, and it is particularly in the early part of a play that a scene may embody character, facts, and purpose, their specific use a pleasurable surmise to the spectator, and under the absolute control of the dramatist.

He forges the chain of events in the way that shall best present what the act in hand requires and what best binds the acts past and to come.

What is to be acted and what may be told is of importance. Indeed, in the exigencies of dramatic economy some one thing may be left to the voice and the manner of the actor, just as to the scenery, and to the intelligent, active thought of the spectators no little can be confided. It is certain that a cause of action or of suffering, if our sympathies or understanding must have some proof, cannot be placed in words only.

The scenes that prove that Jean Renaud, in "A Celebrated Case," is an innocent convict, are imperative. On the other hand, in an adaptation of "Martyr," by the same author, D'Ennery, a prologue is prefixed in order to show that the Italian adventurer and his sister are miserable creatures of degraded and penniless origin — absolutely unnecessary to the last letter and dot, for the simple fact that they were adventurers was entirely sufficient. Their doings in the story were proof of that. Where we expect a certain event in a play to happen, where it must have happened by all the logic of the action, and where to witness it would only delay the progress, it may be told in words. The messenger from the battlefield is an old friend by adoption from the Greek drama. Thus in "Richelieu," Scene I, Act III., François relates stirring and vital happenings to the Cardinal. The dramatic quality of the situation has much to do with it, as where in "The

Daughter of Roland" Marie describes the battle from her outlook at the casement. It is in the apparently small things that doubt and danger arise. Even where the fact is to be put into evidence by action, it remains to determine the effect. In point of time a moment may be enough; and again it must be urged by various devices to the point of absolute impression and conviction. You may have to justify, qualify, elaborate, or restrict it—in order to get proportions, or to provide motives and effects present and future. Peril must be augmented here; character developed there. This must be done, not only for clearness, in order to destroy possible doubt or misapprehension, or no apprehension at all, but to supply interest. The links of the chain must not be defective anywhere.

The thing told differs, or may differ, from the same thing represented. In the one case you deal with the imagination of people of varying powers; in the other you reduce it to a common denominator. Instead of fancy you have fact. Your dramatic incident belongs to you if acted. If acted, it is like putting your evidence before the court. But this needed fact may best be remembered by the ear, the reason, the eye, or the sympathies. It is safe to say that a play should be intelligible to a spectator exclusive of the words; consequently we must assign the very first importance to the visible part of a drama. The gist of it is, that wherever possible and proper, physical expression should be given to an idea. Symbolize all matters of importance. The drama is made up of picture and text.

A writer is often misled by a scene that touches him. He is loth to relinquish it. It is mastery over one's personal fancies of this kind that is the best strength and safeguard of the dramatist. Mr. Bronson Howard relates a curious experience with his "Banker's Daughter," known in England as "The Old Love and the New." Changes had been made in the version of "Lilian's Last Love," the original of the play, but a scene had been retained at the end of the second act, a little girl in its mother's arms, and the tempter bowing his head in the presence of innocence. Something seemed to be wrong in the effect. Its accustomed touch was not in it. It was not until the nineteenth rehearsal at the Union Square Theatre, New York, under Mr. A. M. Palmer's direction, that the scene was entirely omitted. Under the alterations the child and the scene had lost their dramatic functions. It is easy enough to be beguiled by a scene, but in the end the scene and the play alike may lose value.

The moment a case is proved it is enough—be it by scene or act.

Action requires everything that is expressed in the text to be entirely pertinent, and that this is so may be illustrated and proved by its corollary that all acting must express the text or situation only. It is not permissible for an actor to do unnecessary things. An actress has a rose in her hand, for example. If she throws it aside without reason, she expresses something. She has no right to express a thing that does not belong to the part.

The purpose of a scene being fixed, the composition of the scene should be severely governed by it. This would seem to be an easy matter, but the dramatic writer of small experience is misled by the ease with which he can manufacture conversation. Talk by the yard may be spun out, and it may be witty, characteristic, and even "dramatic," and yet not be to the purpose, or have relative value. To leave the mere writing of the scene to the last, until every detail of action has been mapped out and proportioned, is a helpful curb to the facile pen.

As an example of purpose in scenes note "The Honeymoon." At the close of an act will be observed a short scene in which, at a rustic dance, the Duke and Julia appear. It serves to recall the flow of the story, as they had been absent from the stage for a while. "The Honeymoon" is a play that defies the common rules of dramatic construction; but it is amply clear, and the saving force of device is to be seen in the case cited.

A scene being distinct from other scenes, except as it prepares for them, or grows out of them, it has a structure of its own, reproducing in smaller degrees the technique of play and act, such as beginning, middle, and, in so far as is possible in a continuing action, an end.

It might seem that the principles set forth herein had small part in a play like "The Old Homestead," by Mr. Denman Thompson and Mr. George W. Ryer, which ran for more than three years at the largest theatre in New York City; but it is not so. It has been said that this simple drama, with its many characters introduced by apparent chance, and with its meagre plot, is no drama at all. If it be not a drama, then it has established a new set of principles, for it appeals to the universal heart. In point of fact, there are dramas of many kinds, evolved from various intents. The plot of " The Old Homestead " is perfectly clear and consistent and entirely dramatic. Its unity is the ever present glorification of rural simplicity.

Surely the parable of the Prodigal Son is a drama, and old Joshua Whitcomb's search in the city for his boy is a variation of it. "The Old Homestead" knows nothing of complication of plot; nor should it. It is a play of character and local color, slow but accurate in movement, with purpose in every part of it; organic all the way through. The proof of it is the sustained interest. The so-called farce-comedies are dramas, by courtesy, in the fewest instances. They are invariably wearisome in passages.

It has been a traditional rule of the stage, that a tableau in the beginning and course of the action is not permissible. It is related that Bunn, the manager of Drury Lane, refused, greatly to the rage of the wonderful scene-painter Stansfield, to allow the stage to remain unoccupied for a space, to permit the audience to admire a certain scene after the rise of the curtain. Bunn was right. Scenery does, however, sustain a part in the technique of modern plays that requires frank recognition; but scenery must always be accompanied by action or human expression. Pantomime is drama. Henry Irving, in his production of "Faust," exemplified this by his demoniacal scene on the top of the Brocken and the passing of the villagers across the square to the cathedral.

That the stage should never be vacant is another old tradition, but it may certainly be filled with a pause of suspense.

By the French custom, which is a good working one, the coming and going of a person, servants and mere figures excepted, begins and ends a scene; not because the coming and going so happens, but because the action is thereby developed by bits of progress. To the manager and the actor such divisions give the scope of each rôle. The scene belongs to one actor or more, and it is proper for artistic endeavor, as well as effect, that the actor should have definite opportunities. Such a scene may accomplish more than one purpose. In "A Scrap of Paper," for example, the early scene between Anatole and Mathilde gives character and the relations between the two, and thereafter we expect of them merry banter.

The most important part of a play, for it is the greater part, is carried on in dialogue, with usually but two on the stage. The object is to bring about a contributory result by the opposing or the consenting wills. The dialogue seeks to convince, to prevail on, and to further the action. It is not mere argument as in ordinary life, when the disputants part after convincing themselves only. It must have purpose, and, sooner or later, result. The scene should not leave the persons in the same relative position. Dramatic action cannot be disposed of by blunt and sudden agreements.

Approach to agreement, then divergence from, with variations of emotion, mark the dramatic process. The trend of action is forward, but indirectness and retardation are of the essence of dramatic scenes. The drama could not exist without the expression of this delaying thought and growth of resolve. Note the talks of Brutus and Cassius and the conspirators.

By these variations suspense is supplied, and the inner emotions are brought to view. Unnecessary zigzags of purpose and action are as false as the right process is true. Many scenes are by necessity dialogues; and the presence of others has a disturbing effect. If the scene has a moving part in the future action, it certainly makes a party of the listener to that action. It piles up a burden of necessities. Singularly enough in a pretentiously acted version of "Antony and Cleopatra" the royal lovers were at no time alone.

Dramatic dialogue is the art of conducting action by discourse. Like every other particle in the dramatic structure, it must be shaped according to the laws. It must be organic; but that is not enough. Proportion to purpose is its chief requirement. It must advance the action, or establish some fact, just as the author's design may be, and only a certain time can be given to it. It should be suitable to character in thought and dialect, and with reference to the relations between the people of the play. It is possible that on exalted occasions, when men act with formality toward each other, that they make set speeches, but the rule of life is that great variety marks dialogue. Contrast of thought is its great stimulus. It is carried on not by words alone, but look and gesture of consent, dissent, surprise, and the like; and indeed, the response by interjection and manner is essential to animation. Thus we often see in a printed drama such a line as, "I see you start," "The blush comes to your cheek," "You turn your head," etc. Such actions are answers. If there is not obvious interest in the dialogue between the persons of the scene, it is because the author is directing his talk to the audience. Dialogue—the mainstay of the old Greek drama—contains the essence of the drama, for it includes mute expression as before indicated. Dialogue between two gets over ground rapidly; and, in a general way, the greater the number concerned in the scene, the slower the action—something to be considered in getting the proportions of time. The action of a play is not always physical. Two persons seated can carry on a drama. Nothing need "happen" in the scene.

That which a person in a drama may say is governed by his character and by his relations to the other figures and the action. He should at least not speak contrary to character. He must not talk for the sake of talk or as a representative of the author. His talk must have its bearings. Some of it that does not go to the action proper, and which, in consequence, could be omitted in that relation, is used by the skilled writer to convey local color, character, gayety needed at the moment, diversion, and so on. In short, talk is limited by purpose and effect only.

Conversation is a play on the emotions of actor (and spectator), and displays the motives of the characters; it recalls and suggests; it binds and urges on the action. It must not be a mere firing in the air, however full of character. It must deepen impressions, or have a purpose, or interest us in something connected with the play.

A character or play is described as "too talky" when conversation interferes with the action. Talk can be the life of a drama. Sardou and Dumas are exceedingly "talky," if measured by the long stretches of discourse assigned to individuals. See their plays generally. Note how much space is given to Rochat's own account of his meeting with Leah in traveling. In "A Scrap of Paper," Prosper has a great deal to say in a little descriptive talk of the savages as compared with civilized people. Purpose is bound up in every line of it. His room, which we see in Act II., is filled with collected curios, and it excuses the presence there of Suzanne. It has a great deal to do, besides furnishing color, variety, etc. Note that there is nothing of Sardou in it. It is all Prosper.

It may be required to hold the situation for a while by talk, for various reasons, such as to impress an emotion or motive, or for detail for sincerity or vraisemblance. In a manner, you conceal intent, as in Act. II. of "Article 47." Dr. Coombes says to Mazieres, "So I order you to rise early, take exercise, and do no more gambling." Now if mere mechanism would answer and leave impressions, Mazieres might say, "Bah! I am never idle. Gambling is the hardest kind of work." But the author had his purposes, and so he puts a large speech in his mouth, "What! come, come, I am not able to lie idle. I must busy myself over something. Gambling is mighty hard work, mind you! You sit for hours cramped at a table before the same lamps," etc. By such touches, absolute earnestness and reality are given to characters in even casual talk.

Just as a great deal of talk may be required at times, at others none is possible. The strongest situation may be pantomime.

See the adieu of Brutus to his son. The author leaves to the actor all expression when Brutus is alone in his chair looking the way the sacrifice has been led to death.

Just as the subject controls a play, so the situation may be said to control conversation; but that situation or scene may less concern the mechanics—plot—of the play, than it does character, color, surroundings, or some other purpose. It must be within the focus of the play. It must contribute to the illusion.

It is a false practice to make allusions to matters outside the atmosphere of the drama. Certain lighter forms of the stage are privileged, but it is bad art in plays of purpose and life-illusion. Racine and Corneille did not even permit comparisons. Shakspere, however, is full of them. His drama is poetic enough to stand against the canon. Allusions to things of local and temporary significance are at least causes of early antiquity in a play.

Asides, or remarks aside, may be used as a device. They are natural and common enough in life. They only appear artificial when actors are clumsy in conducting a dialogue where they serve to convey to the spectator what is in the mind of the person using them. They are a part of the machinery of comedy. An aside when not intended for the people on the stage should not be observed by them. It is sometimes a material part of the action and then its observance affords such business as may be assigned to it. The monologue is not regarded with favor by the French school of dramatists, but it is a useful device. In point of fact in some of the French classical dramas the dialogues are really monologues uttered in rivalry. The monologue is often clumsily used, but in supreme moments it is entirely natural. Drama is life, and men make their most serious resolves in solitude and alone. When this meditation takes the form of soliloquy, as with Hamlet, the inner secrets of the soul are revealed. The monologues of Richelieu are highly effective. It is a useful device for direct movement. In comedy, and more particularly in farce, which is largely artificial, the monologue is distinctly serviceable. In the more serious drama a restful point is often reached by the monologue.

Monologue should be naturally uttered, and not as for the information of the audience, although that is its object.

It surrenders to the spectator the secrets of the character, and it may lead to an immediate something in the action by being overheard by a figure in the play. Thus the monologue is by no means a mere artificiality. At the same time it should not be used with frequency, and better not at all except where the nature of the case is entirely favorable. It is obvious that as a matter of fact under certain conditions one would not indulge in monologues; what he would say to himself in his chamber, he would not utter in the market-place.

In speaking of monologue a statement may be made that applies to all utterance. We only know what a person in the play thinks by what we see in him and hear from him, or very, very plainly infer. He must express himself, and at the moment. Subsequent explanation is not in the true method of the drama. The sympathy, attention, and understanding belong to the moment. All art is expression, and for a character to feel and not express is absurd.

Groups—unknown to the Greek—necessarily belong to the modern drama, with its large scope of life. The presence of three or more persons on the stage introduces at once the picturesque element, and it becomes the dramatist's care to give employment to all these people. Much of the business for them is commonly left to the stage management, but all the moving to and fro, and all the animation, should be in the author's mind, for pantomime, as already indicated, has its share in dramatic composition. The ensemble scene, or the group, has a large object, impresses partly by its picture and involves energy and action, and commonly prepares or closes a situation that binds together the common action. The use of masses is from special cause and not by general rule. The disposition and management of the mobs and the combats may in its details be left to the practical exigencies of rehearsal. In plays that concern an uprising of the people, or in historical dramas, masses are essential. Great political things are not done in a corner. How to divide masses into groups, how to distribute color and appeal to the eye, how, in short, to bring to your dramatic product the aid of all the arts, is not altogether the scope of this book. It is true that an author should also be equal to stage management; but he may properly call on help at this point.

An episode is an interruption of the action, or

standing still. The episode must concern some element in the piece, or it is a mere interruption. A true episode cannot come from without. It has its uses, as where Brutus, in "Julius Cæsar," has the boy to play the harp for him in his tent in the calm of the night before the battle of Pharsalia. Denman Thompson's "The Old Homestead" is made up almost entirely of episodes, scenes that could be left out without impairing the action, such as the marching along the streets of the band of the Salvation Army. An episode may be used for sentiment, color, a point of rest in the action, and for other reasons. It is abused by feeble dramatists who have a poor subject, or who are unable to exploit a good one. Episodic dramas—to which class belong "The Old Homestead," etc.,—have little of the mathematics of dramatic art in them. It is a bad episode that suspends the interest or that does not permit the action to be resumed without a jog to the memory and the attention. The episode frequently causes disproportion.

Young writers are misled by the beauty of a scene. They conceive it and are loth to give it up. It may not be essential; but as an episode it comes in to the injury of the play, however effective it might be in its right relations. The fact that it is a beautiful scene may be the very reason it should not be there. The gist of all this is, that the drama proper will not suffer padding; and the author will do well, the moment he finds himself disposed to pad, to question his theme more closely. He will find something wrong either in it or in himself.

The skilled writer goes so far into detail that he writes with reference to the "business" of the actors. Business includes those helpful doings that extend, modify, or illustrate the written word; or, it is added by the author as essential where text is best withheld. Beyond a certain point the author's business should not go, and beyond a certain other further point it cannot go, for the actor is entitled to freedom in his methods of expression. Sardou pushes his control of a play to the limit. His notes are not mere suggestions, but express the definite will of a master of his craft.

And yet for the young author to worry himself about stage details, when he knows nothing about them, is absurd. There is a deal of information that it would be useless to give in a book of this character. This is a book of principles. The part of the author is the human part, and has primarily nothing to do with the flies, the "raking piece," the "float," the "backing," the "drop," or with directions as to "lights full up," "blue and white limes off slowly," "lime-lights of blue medium on," etc. How thunder is made, descriptions of the moon-box, the duties of the advance agent and of the manager, the functions of the bill-poster and the mysteries of "three-sheet," the imperturbable grimness of the back-door-keeper, the peculiarities of the box-office man, and the like information, the man who looks to principle in the drama rejects as belonging to the hodge-podge of trivialities that some imagine to be knowledge.

An author necessarily leaves a large margin of expression to the actor and to the stage-manager. The play belongs to the author up to the point of execution. Belot, in "Article 47," gives as a stage direction, "Cora opens her fan calmly." He esteemed this pantomime as essential to his meaning as the accompanying words. Who more competent to suggest the "business" of the play than the author? It is true that an experienced stage-manager understands that better than the unpracticed author; but it is no common thing to witness stupidity in this branch of stage work.

When Claudio, supposed to have been beheaded, throws aside his cloak and rushes to the welcoming arms of his sister Isabella, whose virtue had saved him, have we not seen the genius of Shakspere come to naught because in all the brilliant court surrounding the duke there was no air of joy, of sympathy, of suspense?

Ordinarily the stage-manager is a supplemental author. His first quality should be fidelity to the dramatist. Him he represents in the fullest sense, and should not undertake a production until he has placed himself in entire possession of the general intent of the play and the remotest relations of all its parts. Identity of sympathy and knowledge can alone bring about a just result.

This point mastered, the stage-manager's preliminary duties begin. To state it by practical suggestion, he has prepared a "scene plot," which in some cases is accompanied by models for the machinist and carpenter, or drawings to be followed by the painter, the stage setting and general arrangements being indicated. He has written out a "property plot," so that every article required may be at hand in the proper time, for which his subordinates are responsible. He has indicated the costumes. He has furnished the cues for the incidental music. The gas-man has been instructed as to the disposition of lights. In his prompt-book every incident that can be formulated has been written down—all the "business" of crossing, the entrances, positions, and exits which the actors must follow.

This part of the work finished, it remains to be seen if the stage-manager can execute what his imagination, sympathies, and knowledge have reduced to an almost mathematical basis. If he be equipped at all points, his most delicate task then begins. He is governed largely by his material. The dramatic art—authorship, acting, and stage management—may be summed up in one definite and comprehensive principle—the production of desired effects, in which there must be unity of purpose in the three branches indicated, based on the author's conception.

Accurate "business" is not to the purpose if the actors, in part or in whole, be non-conductors of idea. In this case the author suffers, but it is possible to preserve the proportions of the play to a great extent by accommodating the business to the actor if he cannot be bent to the business.

The movements that we see on the stage, such as crossing from one to the other side, are very often intended not to be specially significant at the moment, but they place the actors in positions for more important movements—it may be merely for an exit. It is the moving of figures on a chess-board with a view to decisive action. We see this in "A Scrap of Paper," at the end of Act I., where the stage direction is, "The party gradually prepare to go out." Sardou does not intend to leave Suzanne and Prosper alone when she demands the compromising letter. The conversation is in low tones, and the woman's action is to be delicate, determined, and piquante, because of the element of danger in the presence of others, for the Baron in a moment is to turn with, "Are you coming, you two?"

To rise and to sit is not always intended merely for variety and movement. The effect in emotion is expressed at times better in one way than the other. In the first interview between Louise and Prosper, her old admirer, Louise is directed by Sardou to sit and take up some embroidery. Obviously that she may halt in the composure of her work and drop the frame when she learns that the letter written three years before was never delivered, and suspects that it may be still in the statue of Flora. A delicate and minute point is thus gained. When Prosper rises in speaking of the looks of the room, it is that his action in going to the statue may not be too sudden. Action has a graduation like that on the canvas of a painter. Every important change of idea should be accompanied by movement—rising, crossing, or what-not.

Effects should never be too sudden. The audience must always slightly or even fully be in advance of the action.

Why does Sardou direct that the shawl of Louise shall be a "remarkable" one? Let us see. Her husband, the Baron, is won over in the second act from his suspicion by Suzanne, and he sits—properly, for he is composed, and his next movement requires emphasis—at the table. He turns and perceives the shawl, and again becomes violent. He should have let his hand wander over that way unconsciously, and thus have directed the attention of the audience to what was coming.

The rightful importance of an author's stage direction may be seen in the same play. When the letter—the "scrap of paper"—is found, Suzanne is seated as if asleep, Prosper admiring her, and congratulating himself that the letter is safe, when she wakes up, apparently, with a sudden start. Sardou directs that Suzanne watch him "with the corner of her eyes."

Thus the audience enters into the arch pleasantry of her triumph, and the scene does not belong so much to Prosper. The audience must always have its share.

Scenes of like character should not be repeated, on account of monotony, and because in a manner the action is brought to a halt, and similar devices should not be used with frequency, such as the reading of letters, etc.; but in the same scene distinctness of idea may require the accent of repetition.

Whatever is needed for an effect it is right to do, but it must not fall short or be in excess. Some effects cannot be accomplished by an outline, but must be minute; others are sufficiently reached by suggestion. It often happens that an incident in an early part of the play comes into true value later on at a remote point. The necessity of making it impressive is obvious. A play is like knitting—it has its back stitches. In the dropped stitch lies the weakness.

The degree of detail to be given to a scene depends on the object of the scene. It may require to be worked out very minutely. Again, a suggestion is enough. What is in a scene should be essential. Unnecessary detail is vicious. We want life, but art must govern its use. The true idea is to give as much of life as you possibly can.

A matter of great importance to be borne in

mind by the author in writing a scene is that the essence of the drama is the present—the moment of the visible, of the physical acting and speaking of the words on the stage; and that present reference as it advances to something that happens within the two hours or more of the duration of the play. Everything must belong to the action; and any reference to anything outside of those limits must have a very, very strong bearing on the actual problem in hand to be admitted at all. The past is absolutely nothing unless recited in order to explain or lead up to something—feeling or fact.

There should be a sequel to every scene. An instance in point is when in "Damon and Pythias" a scene closes with Damon about to hurl his slave to death over the cliff, because he had slain his horse in order to prevent his return to his friend on the scaffold. In a succeeding scene Damon rushes on, saves his friend, but in the tumult even of the situation, he tells of abandoning his fell purpose with the slave as he saw a horseman, and so on.

The number of persons in a scene affects its use and handling. There must be something for everybody to do.

Scenery plays no small part in the economy of the modern drama. It is well enough when the principle is observed that *the scenery should be organic with the play, and should never by imperfection destroy illusion.* A scene may be imperfect by reason of over-elaboration. It may be imperfect because a mechanical effect, however ingenious, may give undue proportion to it. The human interest in a play recedes as the scenic is pushed forward beyond its subordinate limits; but there are so many forms of "plays" that a limit is reached where it is pretty much all scenic display. The mechanical effect is only for the moment. Scenery can only be a background. If the scenery is going to do the acting there is small showing for the human element. It is possible that great quantities of scenery may serve for an organic effect, and we hear of productions like "The Lord Harry," by Henry Arthur Jones and Wilson Barrett, that require six hundred and fifty tons of scenery!

In the face of this possibility, the most powerful of plays may require the simplest of accessories. The rule that has been given seems to cover the case. At all events it shall save space in the matter. The unpracticed writer demands frequent changes of scene. It has been noted that the French dramatists use but one mechanical scene to the act, and that the English method in good practice admits of three by the use of the front scene. It would be the top notch of absurdity to have costly mechanical scenes devoted to brief incidents of small moment. The result would be a phantasmagoria of color or inanimate images, that by their impression on the memory would confound all purpose of the action. Limitation in the scenery is very needful in every way. Again, let it be repeated, the organic and the effective are the right of the drama. If Hamlet walks across the snow-covered rampart, leaving the imprint of his snow-flecked shoes in the powdery substance, or the Ghost glides by without sound and without token of touch, let it be. Stage management may do much for an author, but not all things. Thousands can be, and often are, spent on a play that is not worth a penny.

Everything in a drama tends to the perfect, so that no decorative or dramatic scenic effect should be tried if it cannot be accomplished with full effect. In that case it may be suggested subordinately. It is within the power of stage craft at this time to respond to demands that were once not dreamed of. The falling in of the temple when the pillars are pulled down by Samson in the play used by Salvini could be made wonderfully realistic. The reverberations of sound, the confusion of crashing blocks of stone, the dust obscuring the scene for a moment, and many horrid incidents of the tragic event could be placed in evidence. Good things have been done in this way of recent years. It is a matter of judgment and experience. Bronson Howard in preparing the war effects in "Shenandoah" went on the theory that the sound of combat, the distant roar of cannon, aided by the suggestion of retreating men drawing a cannon, their courage revived by the dashing in of an officer on horseback, a scene of signaling from a mountain-top, and other incidents, were better than a visible conflict.

He was right. A French writer says that a ball-room scene is impossible. Perhaps a battle is also impossible, though much has been done in that direction by the use of figures, etc. These things, usually conceded to stage management, are properly in the province of the author except as to the execution.

Change of the pictorial scene in the course of an act is against the custom of the French dramatists. They have the curtain to fall and dispose of the action in a tableau. Thus there may be ten or twelve tableaus in a five-act piece, and reckoning by interruptions to the action they are so many acts. There is a loss as well as a gain in this method. The English stage has long used the device of front scenes. A pictorial curtain is dropped, or the flats are moved up from the sides, leaving space behind for the arrangement of the succeeding scene. The illusion may be disturbed by this, particularly when objects have to be removed by supernumeraries before the scene is withdrawn. Moreover, the sound of the hammer—which should no more be heard there than in the building of Solomon's temple—makes itself known in the preparation that is going on. The front scene need not be a mere device, a makeshift to gain time for the carpenter, but it often is, and when it is, there being small opportunity and room for effects and large action, the dialogue must be entertaining. Two full scenes, with a front scene interposing, are enough in one act to tax the mechanical help of the stage with. Multiplicity of scene is bad anyway; but by the French method the material is often enlarged beyond its right in order to accommodate the conventionally limited scenery. When the pictorial part is too elaborate, necessitating long delays between the acts, the play may be buried under its tons and "car-loads" of painted canvas and lathe.

The absurdities and difficulties of changing scenery in the course of an act have led to the use of boxed interiors, where an entire act is played in an inclosed room or space.

But the drama is free and will break such bonds. The dramas of life are not acted in parlors only.

The darkening of the stage for the change seems to accomplish what the curtain does for the French tableau; while revolving scenes have accomplished something also.

Still, front scenes are to be avoided wherever they involve absurdity. When the audience is ready for the sequence of the action delay is more detrimental than a quick and skillful change. Imagination is the strong element in illusion, and can stand the English—the Shaksperean system.

Stage management has new problems all the time. The use of electricity has introduced the evil of shadows—which should never interfere. Under any system of lighting, "lights up" and "lights down" are customarily too frequent and too sudden. Irving has solved the difficulty in the appearance of flatness in the scene, by not lighting from the front. One of the chief endeavors of scenery should be to get away from the look of paint.

The pictorial scene must have human sentiment or thought connected with it. A mountain, or a practicable pump, or a shipwreck, or an earthquake cannot act of themselves.

The inanimate can only have an accidental

contact with man in the matter of action. The inanimate is valuable for impressions; and it may go a step beyond that and furnish a moment of influence in the progress of the story. It is necessarily subordinate.

When the mechanical part of the scene enters into the action, it is subject to the same laws that govern action.

For instance, on the first representation of "Elaine," at the end of an act the barge bearing the body of the blameless Lily of Astolat is seen approaching, and the curtain drops before it arrives at the palace steps. The second representation saw this remedied. The barge reaches its destination.

Shakspere can be played without scenery, because of the genius with which the imagination is invoked; but it must be remembered that his plays were written in direct view of the absence of scenery. His dramas, however, admit of scenic luxury. To a modern audience the description of Imogen's chamber would be risked in the absence of all correspondence with the words; Imogen was not wholly neglected—a king's daughter—and deserves well of the stage-manager.

Change of scene is absolutely necessary in certain forms of the drama; but the inexperienced writer has a fondness for changing the scene whether necessary or not. Scenery for the sake of scenery is vicious.

Over-elaboration leads to absurdities. A "notable" production of "Romeo and Juliet" yielded to the prevalent mistaken fancy for what is very often preposterous detail of magnificence and effect. Never was better proof of the managerial fallacy that mere costliness counts in the drama.

Juliet's room was a nest of splendor. The paternal care of the manager for this delicate daughter of the Capulets induced him to provide her apartment with comfort in the way of a large fireplace, something that would indicate that he sympathized with the "cold day" that was about to break in on the lovers. He heeds not the remonstrance of the nightingale and disdains the joyous notes of the lark. Geographical propriety must give way to the cheerful blaze. It is a merry flicker that the light plays on the fatal scene, and the aristocratic dog-irons glint with ruddy contentment at the fire fed by backlogs and abundant hickory; while those of a domestic turn in the audience regret the absence of a tea-kettle to sing its love ditty. A broom could well nestle in the corner, and commend the tidiness of one whose tragic end denied her the completion of housewifely instincts. A day of wicked weather it must have been in this manager's Verona.

Realism is a proper application of scenic and mechanical illusion. There is a false realism where the scene itself is pushed into an importance that is not sustained by the play. There is a false realism where the action is utterly out of taste. The frankness—that is, the naturalism—of Zola does not introduce new principles into the drama, which has always been realistic as well as ideal. Realism is all right if it realizes, and is all wrong if it does not. Naturalism, that which an author contributes to a play, and realism, that which the actor and the stage-manager contribute, are one in spirit; it being a mere question of terms.

The burden of expression in the old school was the actor. It was an individual affair with him. He required the centre of the stage, and there was a general tendency toward the footlights. It was the man, almost to the entire exclusion of accessories.

Henry Irving's methods put action largely in the middle distance. The genius of himself and company was not impaired, however, when they acted without scenery, as they did at West Point. Indeed, no scenery at all is better than bad or inappropriate scenery, and if the human interest is strong enough, the imagination completes the illusion.

Irving's scenery was never merely spectacular. It was never useless. He is a great stage-manager—a man of ideas. Witness " Faust." Was there ever such economy of powerful means in such an exciting scene as the Carnival on the Brocken? This turmoil has a very short duration—certainly not more than ten or twelve minutes. The very means used are magical. The shifting of the figures is inextricable to the eye. Nothing is repeated. The thundering sounds and multiplied crashes are distinct in every horrid whisper and consummated terror of discord; the witch flying across the abysm of the suddenly lighted heavens, the rising of the moon, the jubilant but weary climbing of the first figures, their disappearance, the easy descent and triumphant presence of Mephistopheles with Faust straggling behind him; the sudden emptiness of the scene recalling the fact of the blasted nature of the mountain-top; then the throng trooping in with weird song, the apes and bats climbing the dead trees, the dance of the demons, the wailing history of the old crone who has traveled in vain for three hundred years; the imp forging sparks of blue light from the rock where is seated Mephistopheles, the lustful winningness of the mute female suitors of Faust, who carry him aside from view, and the final clash of disappearance—are wonders of imaginative work. The secret is as much in the detail of conception as in the execution. It is authorship itself, this use of scenery.

CHAPTER VI.

CHARACTER AND CHARACTERS.

THE persons of a drama are significantly called characters, and so strong is the necessity for distinctness in their respective functions, that we find Phillip Massinger supplying his "A New Way to Pay Old Debts" with Sir Giles Overreach, Wellborn, Allworth, Justice Greedy, Marrall, Tapwell, Froth, Amble, and Furnace. His play in simplicity and power of construction is a model. His art is far in advance of the crude day when the characters were straightway named after the cardinal virtues and vices that they stood for. There was no need of the device with him, but it strikingly illustrates the principle that a dramatic character must be distinguished by a prevailing trait, purpose, and use in the action. At present, art is felt to be a little closer to life in not making use of this device while it continues to use the principle. It was only another form of the same thing when in the time of carefully governed stock companies the lines of business were closely drawn by the actors. The irascible old man, the walking gentleman, the low comedian, and all the other specialists went their way secure in the assignment to them of fitting parts in the play.

Character is to be studied out in detail by the author just as carefully, and by means of notes, as he has worked out the plot and developed the acts and scenes. It requires a special meditation of its own.

The brief action of a drama and art itself rejects a multitude of non-essential things, but in effect it is possible to reproduce character on the stage, with an illusion that is practically perfect. What we know as the character of a man is after all the general knowledge of that man. He is good, bad, generous, miserly, brave, or craven, as the case may be. He is what he oftenest appears to be. He is what he proves himself to be in the affairs in which he is an actor. If we hold to the principle that the drama is life, we find no mystery in the creation of character; but the drama has certain laws of its own, so that Overreach and Greedy and Wellborn must maintain their character so far as the audience is concerned from the first to the last. This does not exclude the facts and truth of life, for in the mimic action he may appear to his associates to be one thing and surprise them by being another.

When, therefore, it is said that a character must have dramatic unity, it is absolutely true with reference to the audience. Dramatic unity, then, is the first essential of a character. It is proper to repeat, as was repeated with reference to acts and scenes, that the general laws govern every detail. We can, for example, no more force an immoral character to acceptance as an immoral character, than we can find success with a bad moral object for a play.

Only those sides of a character that promote the action are required in a play. The shorter the time of performance, the greater the complication of plot, the larger the number of persons directly concerned, the more general the treatment. The play of character admits of more detail subject to the principles stated. The reserve of common knowledge of any class of men permits of effective work in few strokes. Witness Shakspere's Old Adam in "As You Like It," and the Apothecary in "Romeo and Juliet," while Massinger's Tapwell and Froth are perfect impressions. It is in the early part of the play that the foundation for character is laid. There, too, the helping incidents may have a minuter touch, for the action of a more exacting kind prevails later on. In plays of any kind, character should be revealed at the earliest moment. As to characters in general, the audience wishes to soon single out and to know the chief object of sympathetic attention. Expectation of what is to come is largely fostered by this.

Character is not created by what is said of a person by others; but it may be prepared and confirmed by these side-lights. The character must be witty, or brilliant, or generous, independent of any description. The methods and conditions of Shakspere's plays permitted more of this contributory matter than the modern drama. These touches need not be absent. If integral with the action and not an obvious and redundant device, they have the warrant of good practice.

It is the value of a scene, its relativeness and other qualities, that impresses character. The length of a scene may not be prescribed, but care must be taken that sufficient time be given to it, not too much or too little. It is certain that a word will not fix it. It is certain that the consent of the audience must be got for all that is done. The character must have probability, or, better said, actuality, and adequate motives. No artificiality of reasoning or plot can compensate for their absence. When this structural weakness exists, the author usually has some explanation stuck away somewhere in the text; but that is mechanism, and not after the natural, generous, and yet stern laws of the drama. It is not the number of lines spoken that creates character, nor the fact that they are in character as they should always be, but their use.

Mere incidents of character amount to nothing unless they have to do with the action, and are apt to make the character diffuse, or to weary by reiteration. All things in a drama work to the common good, and a character may draw aid from every adjunct of the stage. Just as action and the tone of a piece may be influenced by the scenery, so may a character take a color. The home of a man proclaims him: the sybarite in his chambers, the pauper in his hovel. Thus, there are so many things contributory to character on the modern stage that the text plays a smaller part than it did when words were the chief means of expression. The writer must settle with himself how far he shall make his play literary or practical. The word is often essential; repetition is often required for character as well as plot, as where Jean Renaud's "hot temper and jealousy" is referred to frequently in the identical phrase, without a single manifestation of it. A definite technical purpose apart from mere character covers the case. The real character affects the action and is affected by it. That is the test as to the real and the incidental. Thus character is an integral part of all that is done. The actor imagines that he creates a character, whereas its composition has in it elements that lie far away from anything that is in his function or power to do.

He helps to create it; so does the audience, so does the author; and where the illusion of a noble character is perfect, there is a divine something in it that no man can lay sole claim to. External characteristics, such as dress and personal expression, the actor must needs supply. He interprets, and indeed he may add something of his own. One actor may express a character by the use of few words; another may be inadequate to the same part, and to that one a fuller text might be given. When a character is strongly local, and of a period, like Sir Pertinax Macsycophant, no words alone can effect results.

There are many forms of the drama, and they are distinguished by the relative proportion of their elements. The character play, as a study of character, has its place only as one of them. The general laws of dramatic character remain for all of them.

The real action of a play is carried on by few

persons, though it may require the presence on the stage of many.

Characters are created for purposes belonging to the action in proper function. In " Camille," Armand's father is in it for a great scene; an act, and then he is retired. A false tendency of technique would have him in at the death. An instance of created character and purpose is that of Poncelet in " Eustace Baudin "—note page 41 of the play.

The number of characters in a play depends upon the necessities of the action. Characters of the real movement are few. " Caste " has seven and a servant. In many plays the number could be fewer, as far as mere action is concerned, but largeness of life requires numbers. They are needed for color, breadth, and variety. The drama has expanded since Horace wrote: "Let not a fourth person speak."

For an example of the use of incidental characters and of a scene for color and atmosphere examine page 4 of " Daniel Rochat." Voltaire's room and the curiosity or ignorance of strangers does not concern the movement of the story.

Sardou's use of Dr. Bidache is noteworthy. He identifies him with the main character, Daniel Rochat, and thus gets over philosophic ground without monotony.

The star actor wishes to obtain the chief share

in pieces written for him, and thus proportions are sometimes disarranged. There is an evil in this, but in plays written for stock the interest should not be too scattered.

The dramatic author reaches a certain limit, and cannot impart character, in so far as his manuscript goes, to a mere incidental figure, such as the servant. It is to the actor that he looks to mark the figure with class distinction. Incidental figures may be introduced into a play at any time that the action calls for them. They may be of decisive importance, and be full of character, but they are to be recognized as incidental. Martin, Sister Genevieve, and many others, are striking incidental figures in "The Two Orphans." Nothing is unimportant in a play. Perfection is the watchword of the drama. A good play should not be done on the installment plan. Every character should be played up at the same performance. A subordinate figure should always be played well. If it is not, why, there you have mechanism and disillusion in its baldest form. Too often has an audience been invited to ribald jest by the appearance of the soldiers of the Grand Army of the Roman Republic. With minor characters we should at no time be in doubt; and they, as all characters, should do, and be expected to do, only what has been promised for them by their dramatic sponsors. There should be no useless characters, but under certain conditions mere lay figures give breadth of life and local color to a piece. As a rule, a character that does not contribute to the action proper is a nuisance— as unwelcome as the unbidden guest at the wedding-feast.

It is not enough to say that a person of the drama must have unity of character. It must also have unity of function. The economy of a play requires that two characters should not be used to do what may be accomplished by one.

Play-writing is analysis by common sense, and, so practiced, it is not misled by false interpretation of principles. To illustrate, the principle is in no degree violated by the first and second murderer in "Macbeth," or by Rosencranz and Guildenstern in "Hamlet." A drama admits of but one hero, for in him is bound up the unity of the action. The double heroes like Romeo and Juliet are common enough, but they glow together like the binary star.

It may be said that humor in the drama is provided rather by character and situation than by the literary expression. In farce it is largely brought about by ridiculous complications and incident, and by mechanical process. In comedy, which is close to life, it is the commonplace happening that most excites laughter. The henpecked husband, the bashful lover, and familiar types, furnish its best supply.

Aristotle gives it as a rule that the character of a hero, in order to gain our sympathy, should be made up of mixed evil and good. Whatever may have been the bearings of this maxim on the Greek drama, which dealt in demigods or characters of tradition, it is true to-day when the drama is human and filled with passion. It is certain that in these times the hero must be human and not repulsive, and must have motives that commend themselves to our reason. His history must entertain us. Shakspere reconciles us to Iago by that honest gentleman's wit and causes of action. Lessing discusses very fully Aristotle's elements of tragedy, such as pity, terror, and horror. To his "Dramaturgie" the matter may be referred. For modern practical use, the element of taste, æsthetics, is decisive.

It may be repeated here that while all the characters should, if possible, be introduced or foreshadowed in the first act, it is not a set rule. If it were, we would hear of the Miss Bloomfields before page 32 of "Daniel Rochat," and of Charles Henderson before Act II. But it is bad art to withhold a principal character too long.

It was once the rule to reunite all the characters in a circle before the footlights, and close the play with a tag spoken by the chief person, and often with a succession of lines by each. This arrangement, particularly in artificial farce, had artistic reasons for its use, but it has no universality of application. True art tires of conventionality, and we find in late plays, such as "Fernande," by Sardou, only three characters on the stage when the final curtain falls. In the play twenty-five persons figure.

Aristotle says that character must be agreeable, decent, reasonable, and consistent. It may be added that it is effected by motives, speech, action, and external tokens.

These attributes cover many things. Their disobedience could be illustrated by many examples by way of warning. It might be said that the hero of a play should not be placed in an unworthy situation or dishonored, but that would simply repeat the law that character should be consistent and maintained.

We have already seen that the stage is not opposed to vice in character, but it does not permit smallness in persons of interest. This does not require them to be perfect. On the contrary, the drama is possible only by reason of human errors.

It has been already stated that character in dialogue is not in itself drama.

Characters must act by free will. That is to say, they must have motives, or they become puppets. They are also mechanical when they speak for the author and not for themselves. Having motives, they must do what is expected of them.

If two rivals, for instance, appear in the presence of the object of their love, or of one whose good or evil will concerns them, the situation must evoke character. Character is not to be dropped at any moment, for that matter, but there must be no situation where inactivity is worse than negation. The character must be sustained if established, confirmed if suggested.

Character in part or full should be seen at once. The first words should proclaim it if the trait is to play a part of importance. An illustration of this is to be found in "Eustace Baudin," where the first talk is of eating. Later on in the play this apparent trifling comes into the reckoning.

A character is sustained by happenings in which he is not seen in person. It is a matter of keeping the factor in mind. The value of the person as well as the trait has to be kept up.

It is within the lines of true comedy to charge

character at times. It is the same as loading a point with pigment in painting a picture. It must be true in spite of exaggeration. Or, we can reinforce character by an incident. This is best done when a happening dependent on the trait is to follow.

It would require a philosophy of life itself to discuss what is noble in character, and the like. In trying to compass nobility the danger in plays of blank verse has always been bombast. It ensues whenever the character talks of himself. In practical plays taste keeps this defect within control. How character displays itself is for the student of human nature to learn or to know. It is worth while to make one observation: a genuine quality, good or bad, is unconscious of itself. The rascal rarely knows his own turpitude; the vain man sees himself in a rosier light than others do; virtue is not artful; and so on.

The management of the entrance and exit of characters is important. Simple as this may appear to be, there is no detail of the drama that is subject to more bungling. In point of fact it involves important principles—principles that are widely applicable in construction. The scenic circumstance may explain the presence or the coming of a person on the stage, but general character and purpose must, if not known in advance, be made apparent as soon as possible; and, generally speaking, an entrance and an exit must be characteristic. There must be preparation. But naturalness, not excess of device, should govern. It is an old trick of actors that demand attention for themselves to insist on being heard without, by means of song or a bustle of some kind—as much as to say, "I am coming." This is vanity not always pardonable, but it is based on good technique. In making an exit your low comedian will bump up against the wing if he can get emphasis no other way. Thus every act on the stage tends toward the definite. Thus the characters become clear cut, and purpose enters into their doings. Preparation for an entrance may include the reason for the entrance, but reason there must be. A figure should never be retired on the pretext of doing something which he does not do, or something that is immaterial to the action or the character. In the movements on the stage the figure must not be so far from his point of exit that his lines or his business are exhausted before he reaches it. Few experienced actors subject themselves to this absurdity, but it is something for the author to look to as well.

Sometimes a scene that belongs to a certain

character may be so strong and so bound up in the action that that character must be prepared by other means for the spectator than by simple development of its own. In this way indirect creation of character is helpful and needful.

Where it is desirable to give a significant entry to a character, it is obvious that two people of equal interest should not come on together. Of course no rule can be made against an entry together that is at once natural and of advantage to the action.

Contrast of character is important in a technical way, and natural juxtaposition is a necessity. In "Camille," ten or fifteen minutes are given to contrast of character and the like, where Prudence comes to borrow money from the dying Camille. This contrast is a powerful element in making character. It may exist between the situation and the complications, as well as between characters. Systematic and habitual contrast is a bad thing. Consult the subject rather than conventionality.

Stage humor is in a manner distinct from literary humor. It is often not in the lines at all, but in the relation of the actors to each other, or in the situation, as in an anecdote there is much that we know and enjoy not expressed in the telling.

Conventional types are not always to be avoided. They belong to the trade, are staple, and it is only a question of being true to your theme and not being dominated by the conventional.

The use of children is tempting, but not always does it give good results. Shakspere was sparing. Note in "Macbeth" the son of MacDuff; in "Winter's Tale" the boy; etc., etc. Children may be grouped with effect, but as a rule the dramatist should be careful not to confide too much to them.

The comedy of character is so distinctive that some writer has said that it cannot support intrigue. This means that the plot is subordinate. We may see this confirmed by many of the plays written for character actors. They are usually melodramas revamped with the comedy part, an odd mixture in which the play itself is of small consideration. The truth of the matter is, comedy proper is very generous with its characters, and to interest the public in one amusing person only is against its special technique. It is easily possible to write one-part plays, but the work in the way of authorship is commonly done badly, while the actor's part may be perfect.

CHAPTER VII.

A SUMMARY OF CERTAIN LAWS IN ART.

THE drama can borrow instruction and illustration from all the arts. There is hardly a detail in painting that does not apply in some way to the technique of the drama. Composition, color, perspective, climax, proportion, expression, and what belongs to character, background, contrast, tone, clearness, harmony—are a few of the properties in common. For the man who has the instinct of art this suggestion has its value. It is sufficient now to bring together for brief comment a few of the principles that require the distinction of some treatment. They may gain by this repeated emphasis some new aspects.

Mere continuity of incidents is not enough. It is better to break continuity than to be dull. Witness "The Honeymoon."

Perspicuity is a prerequisite for all forms of expression, and is in close agreement with any charm that we experience. An indistinct action is as bad as a blurred picture.

Intelligibility in a play will save many defects. The repetition of an idea is not an infrequent device to this end. In a general way a play should be so clear that one coming late into a theatre may take up the thread of the action.

There is no reason why a playwright at all capable should not at least be lucid. Clearness is altogether a technical quality. It does not appertain to the real merit of the material, which in itself may entirely fail to reach the heart of an audience, or may contain far more than the author has it in him to discover; but what he does know he should be able to tell. Distinctness is also the essence of good acting. The attention of the hearer should be free. To withhold him from sentiment by obscurity in the media of communication is absurd. No well-written play is above the understanding of the boy in the gallery.

The language of a drama should be dramatic and appropriate to character, and it is this requisite that the skilled translator obeys. As a rule, the highest type of the conversational is to be sought. The author could not make a greater mistake than to permit all his characters to talk slang. Slang is fatal to good sense and honest feeling. The dramatist who makes his characters of good station in life talk incorrect English is an inborn vulgarian.

Boucicault's translation of "Led Astray" is a perfect example of the transference from the French to the English of the dramatic qualities in language. Blank verse is essentially dramatic, with its swing, dignity, and adaptability. Short sentences in dialogue are in the nature of quick and progressive action, but occasion arises for very considerable uninterrupted utterance. In all cases the language of the drama, except that of the poetic in verse, and that of the farce, is distinctly the speech of every day, sometimes heightened for cause.

Plainness, or rather effectiveness, is not to be sacrificed for beauty. Verbal obscurity and general opaqueness is an unpardonable sin. There is so much sincerity and simplicity required in the construction of a good play that it may almost be said that only a genuine nature can write one. The language is intended to be understood by everybody, to the uttermost gallery.

Contrast is inevitable in the drama. The opposition of natures brings into relief differences of natures. There is a contrast of motives and of characters, and throughout the play the tendency to put light against shade, color against color, and situation against situation, and so on, is very strong. Note how brightly Lesurques starts in. He is filled with happy anticipations. This tendency to contrast in the drama appears in the text in epigram and antithesis.

Gradation is that wise husbanding of effect that keeps the play at a natural pace. An example of this is Esther's play with the letters in her hand, before telling the contents of one of them to D'Alroy in "Caste." The dramatic idea, on the whole, requires rapidity of movement; but if the movement be too rapid it may easily fall into the artificial. Gradation reins in the movement.

Much in the same way indirectness prevents abruptness, and gives to the action an automobility that relieves it of the appearance of art. For example, a character may be at a certain place for one object, say to meet another person, and while there overhear a conversation that gives a new turn to affairs. Dramatic movement is filled with these new springs of action, these deflections whereby the plot is not in the hands of one character, but is effected by the doings of each.

Proportion goes to many parts of a drama, the force of bits of action, the length of scenes, the

A Summary of Certain Laws in Art. 169

use of characters and effects generally, until in the sum of all we note the perfect result. It is a vital source of beauty. A play is not complete until it is acted, so that dress rehearsals should mark the most important stage of workmanship. Dumas *fils* says that the art is almost wholly a thing of proportions. The values in painting have the same significance as proportion. It applies to all parts of the drama, as, for instance, a scene of great strength usually requires one of corresponding strength in apposition.

Variety as a technical grace in handling material has no small value. It forbids the too frequent use, whenever it is to be avoided, of the same devices in the same play. It counsels against opening the acts with monologues in succession, or by the reading of letters, or whatever may have been used once. The same situation is not to be repeated. Monotony is to be avoided. It is perhaps not altogether necessary, but it is safe to remark that variety in this relation does not countenance the introduction of so-called specialties by performers.

Illusion is the end aimed at by the acted piece, that combination of so many energies and of so many practical appliances. The theatre-goer enjoys the abiding reminiscence of some moments in his experience when he has forgotten his surroundings and believed that what passed before him on the stage was a reality, and not an imitation of a reality. Such an illusion, however, is rarely general in an audience or continuous with the action. It may bring an audience to complete surrender at every point of judgment and sympathy, and leave impressions as lasting as any that life affords. It requires a perfect combination of naturalness and art to bring this about. Any interruption or divergence, accidental, mechanical, or personal, has the illusion at its mercy. Its preservation is the constant problem of stage management, and vigilance at each performance is unceasing; all of which is plain, practical common sense. With what a fine sense of responsibility, then, should not an author proceed in his labors that precede the employment of so many human and mechanical forms! Is he to dash off his scenes in a careless-confident way, without conscientious appreciation of every effect, while a scene-shifter is discharged for the slightest delinquency? Nay, his duty extends further, in two directions, in this day of accuracy and of scenic completeness. He must not leave such opportunities for disillusion as come with the appearance of stage hands in livery or costume to remove the paraphernalia of a scene; nor must he introduce technical mechanism for motives of character and action. He may sin by omission and commission. Probability is the greatest aid to illusion in the poet's part of the work. Probability cannot be created by mere trick. A clear and possibly an elaborate statement of the facts in a given case, but the facts must be true and not false. We will accept the most extravagant things, but not a deliberate dramatic lie. It may be backed up by all manner of subtle reasoning and by all the tricks of the trade, and the lie will not prosper.

A volume could be written recounting improbabilities in dramas. Some of them are impossibilities, but there must be truth in them somewhere. In Schiller's " Robbers," the glowing word and deed of these perturbed spirits of the story carry illusion. Illusion determines probability, and technique has something to say in the matter, for if there is no preparation or no motive the scene is improbable, that is, its artificiality is seen; as where, for convenience, in "The Love Chase," the author has Lydia attacked. It is motiveless, sudden, and ineffective. In certain forms—the farce, for example—there is no such thing as improbability.

Probability depends on the atmosphere of

the play. We accept the disguise of Rosalind in "As You Like It," but not of the woman in Buchanan's "Infatuation." In "Ingomar," which is romantic, we do not care about the geography of Massilia, and nothing for the ethnology of the Allobrogi; nor do we insist too much against the satin slippers and Greek gown of Parthenia in the mountains. The natural things are plain enough; it matters not if there be no real Massilia and no Allobrogi.

In "Eustace Baudin" all sorts of things happen between the acts; first he is confined in a lunatic asylum, and then in prison; but it suits us to admit all the happenings without question. It does not trouble us that the gardener's son in "The Lady of Lyons" could not well have carried on his courtship undetected, but we are ready to excuse if our will goes that way. The revolutionary times have a bearing on it.

Probability depends also on the use to be made of a fact. The audience will consent to what is not in itself probable, but what is possible, if it be properly handled. Again, an improbability in real life may be the most grateful truth in a play of fancy. There would be no play if the hero were to do certain things. The author should show reason why he did not.

Illusion, or sense of reality, may exist in a play however often you may see it. No one thing produces it. It is not a trick. It is compounded of all that enters into a play. Appreciation of the author's art has nothing to do with it, and consequently he is the best critic who for the time being submits to the illusion. He is the best spectator who easily yields. It is perhaps not possible to make one forget for several hours that what he sees passing before him on the stage is an imitation, and believe that it is a reality. And yet that is the object, unattainable as it may be. Schlegel says that the terrors of tragedy would be a torture if we believed in its reality. Very curious conjecture and discussion could spring from that proposition; but it is not practicable to consider illusion any more closely than has here been done.

To create and sustain illusion is of inestimable value to actor as well as author. Where the illusion is not, you see the trick. You observe with curious interest that Edwin Booth's art lies largely in the grace of his hands, or, that with Henry Irving it is thoughtful scholarship applied to detail, and so an illusion is the conjunction of all things that produce reality—the acting, scenery, probability—everything. It requires perfect art in all the branches of the production, scenic as well as acting. Attainable illusion is created when a spectator remembers a scene or a play as if it were an actual experience in his life. Thus Schlegel's apprehension comes to nothing, for you get the moral benefit without the torture.

The fault of disillusion in improbable passages is commonly in the mechanical nature of the action.

Preparation and proof are almost identical with the conduct of a case at law. You state your facts and cause of action, make proof, and ask judgment. We see that Lesurques tells of his father's poverty, the pleasure that he will have in providing for him, etc., etc.

It is not necessary to tell an audience what is going to be done, although in "The Honeymoon" the Duke favors us with his design as to Juliet. In "The Danicheffs" we are not informed that Ossip is reserving Anna for his master, but we have lost sight of them for an act, and the *coup* is successful when it breaks on us. We are not told in advance that D'Alroy in "Caste" is not dead. How to foster anticipation is suggested by the material.

The art of withholding as well as the art of foreshadowing are secrets of the dramatist. So

A Summary of Certain Laws in Art. 175

delicate are the necessities, that to attempt to give rule in these concerns would be to do more than this book promises.

Dubosc comes to his ruin in the last act through his love of the bottle. Note how the point of his brandy drinking is forced in the first act. It is the sign by which he is made known.

In the same play, when Lesurques is under trial, a countryman appears with the spurs that he had lost. The peasant is an incidental character introduced for the first time. It is ample preparation that we know the spurs were left behind. Explanation is often a mere formality, for the audience has divined the case, or finds in the expressed explanation immediate satisfaction.

Expectation is skillfully handled in this way sometimes.

Preparation is of extreme importance. This is something more than assigning motive for actions. There is no time to be explaining the nature of a scene during its progress. There is, for example, a scene of shipwreck. We should be prepared for the import of the scene, the rescue of a certain person, or the like. Preparation includes motive, but motive is something that in scope lies beyond expression at times. Cause must be shown for everything that happens. In the case of murder committed by a villain, his nature is motive enough, but preparation for the specific deed must be made, in order to be dramatic. If an honest man commits murder in a drama, it may require the entire play to set forth his motive or justification. There must always be a reason, whether of sentiment, of judgment, or of the logic of events.

Much might be said of the value of truth—fidelity to nature. Fitzgerald amply illustrates the aberrations from it in modern comedy. Truth applies the rule that all should be done in character.

Suspense is interest awakened to curiosity, and sympathy mixed with doubt as to the result of an action added thereto. It is more than curiosity, for we feel the suspense in familiar plays. We live over old experiences with an interest that may be more tender by repetition. Suspense is the test of the highest interest. Skill may maintain it in a way that tests art. In "Jim the Penman" there are constant interruptions of impending danger. The reappearance of the check, the interviews between Jim the Penman and Baron Hartfeldt, and other passages, keep up suspense constantly. Thus suspense is the holding things in solution, solving nothing as long as that something is of use to the action.

These elements are recalled here to emphasize their necessary presence and close relationship in every play; and to urge upon the author the importance of reviewing and questioning his work, as he proceeds, so as to keep it close to the simple requirements of the drama.

CHAPTER VIII.

ADAPTATION AND DRAMATIZATION.

THE adaptation of plays is not only a proper method of increasing our store of dramas, but it is a resource to which the manager will be constantly driven by practical necessity.

Successful pieces are comparatively rare, and the public demands novelties. There are sentimental objections urged by the upholders of the native drama against the importation of foreign material; but it may be assumed that the manager is not amiss in his liking for the product of writers whose names give assurance of merit and success. A drama by Sardou, Dumas, D'Ennery, Sims, or Pettit, has a commercial value. There is an advertising quality in the brand. If management consisted in simply buying and selling an article just as found in the market, it would be an easy business; a mere barter in literary hogsheads of sugar and sacks of coffee. And indeed, this commercial idea of the case sends many a venture to the bottom.

The manager esteems himself wise in his purchase. He is astute in the use of the means so well known to him in presenting the property to the public. He has courage in the mounting of it. He employs a company at salaries commensurate with the anticipated receipts. In the mean time, by a fatuity hard to explain, he often neglects to have his play put into shape for his market. The failure, for that matter, may proceed directly from the adapter. The work may be badly done, or not be done at all.

In New York, Wallack's Theatre in its latter days was governed by English actors and stage-managers, who reproduced English melodramas untouched, and the house crumbled season after season toward its final disaster. Mr. A. M. Palmer, in his career of ten years as manager of the Union Square Theatre, owed his continuous and uncommon prosperity to his suggestiveness and carefulness in the matter of adaptation whenever it was a question of handling a foreign play. The process of adaptation may be applied to the entirely new and original piece as well as to the imported. Each must be adapted to stage effect. The process was substantially adaptation in the case of Bronson Howard's "Banker's Daughter" as it was with "The Two Orphans." In the one case the whole scheme was changed. In the other the entire last act was dropped.

Ordinarily the adapter, if we may judge by his handiwork so often thrust before us, is a marplot. The power of the piece vanishes, no man knows whither. The manager is astonished that a judicious mixture of robustious horse-play and muscular tragic action engrafted on the elusive play does not accomplish results.

It would seem unnecessary to aver that the mere translation of a drama is something entirely distinct from the art of adaptation. Yet we find a drama by D'Ennery presented without a single mark of intelligent workmanship. To simply recount the story of "Duprez and Son" is to verify this statement. A father who has been untrue to an early love, and has married one of his maturer affections, has in his home and business establishment the two products of his lawful and unlawful alliances, respectively. The legitimate son is the scoundrel who succeeds in turning their common father against the baseborn but noble one. These two natures are in deadly conflict throughout, and only after trials of poverty, blindness, and cruel fortune does the virtuous pledge of an unsanctified love return, with wife and child, to receive the blessing of the repentant old man, who learns of his error of judgment. The legitimate youth is cast into the outer darkness. Possibly a philosophic Frenchman may sympathize with all of the figures in this drama, which is "technically" a fine one; but to expect any man of the English race who is wise enough to know his own father and pure enough to love his own mother, to enter into the spirit of this revolutionary fustian, is a trifle too much. Had the employed adapter mislaid his common sense? The alterations essential to this play are too obvious to dwell upon. It would be a plain and simple task to make it a strong and honest performance. Not so did the always wise and always pure Shakspere treat the same theme in "As You Like It."

Charles Reade scornfully said of the ordinary adaptation: "It is as easy as shelling peas; and I know."

It is obvious that many so-called adapted plays are only translations. Wherever the characters, the names, the motives, the incidents, the whole thing, in fact, remains foreign, it is a translation. Some plays, for that matter, defy adaptation. It is often essential to convert a character into something else; just as the ballet-dancing mother-in-law in "Les Surprises du Divorce" becomes the woman's-rights woman in "The Lottery of Love," by Augustin Daly.

Mere change, however, does not always work well. When the adapter of D'Ennery's "Martyr" substituted a French Corporal for an Indian servant he could not have made a graver mistake. The Indian servant was specially created to keep alive the fact that the daughter had been far away from the unhappy scenes in Paris. Adaptation may require all the skill that an original author must use; and it is often the better skill. The English playwrights are often happy in their work, as witness Robertson, who made of "Caste" and "School" plays of his own and essentially English. By the same process Molière's "Tartuffe" was the remote ancestor of "The Serious Family."

"The Banker's Daughter" was twice adapted, once by Mr. Palmer in New York, and again in London by James Alberry, in conjunction with the author. Mr. Bronson Howard, in a lecture delivered in Boston and printed in four columns of the *Herald* of that city of March 27, 1876, gives a minute account of the necessities of alteration demanded by differences in English and American social habits.

Adaptation is a necessity in proportion to the provincialism of a nation. England is stubbornly narrow, and few pieces are presented in London that have not been subjected to change, in deference to prejudice. In this way has arisen a formidable body of impostors who assume to act as excise officers of the drama, and affix their names to the works of Scribe, Sardou, or any other writer that falls into their clutches, such as "A Scrap of Paper," by Palgrave Simpson, and everything he can lay his hands on, by Sydney Grundy.

The delight afforded by Mr. Joseph Jefferson's Bob Acres cannot be distinctly transmitted by tradition. The country squire in his present form is as real and mortal as our cherished comedian. Less perishable is Mr. Jefferson's service in re-creating the play of "The Rivals." He has swept away the disturbing artificialities of the plot. The only character that has proved to be obdurate is Lydia. Her overwrought sentimental romanticism was a thing of the day, and happens to be as to the play integral; otherwise nature and true proportions exist in Mr. Jefferson's version. The changes that have been made are of the most delicate and skillful description. It will be profitable to dwell for a brief space on the material additions to the comedy.

In a day of such oaths as " 's death's," " 'oons," " zounds," " gad," and " by the Mass," there was a purpose in the novel plan of swearing adopted by Bob Acres, but at the present day there would be small significance in his "odds frogs and tambours," "odds flint and triggers," "odds daggers and balls!" Mr. Jefferson has retained a mere suggestion only of this satirical device.

It is not essential to point out in detail the re-arrangement of scenes in their entirety. Printed in parallel columns, the original text and the new version would show that it is a matter mainly of technical skill in bringing out points, with the addition of matter entirely in character. For example, Bob Acres and his servant David are discovered. David says: "I warrant Dolly Tester, your honor's favorite, would blush like my waistcoat." The new version interrupts with: "I would like to see Dolly—and Dolly would like to see me." He refers to his bravery of attire, and his mind reverts to his simple country home. The original has: "But, David, has Mr. De La Grace been here?" Jefferson puts it, with an obvious gain in clearness and directness: "David, tell the dancing-master to come."

The diverting incidents that follow are new, except that David, according to Sheridan, says: "I can't help looking at your head! If I hadn't been at the cooking, I wish I may die if

I should have known the dish again myself!" The servant goes off content with this comparatively ineffective wit, that has more of Sheridan in it than of David. Our comedian arranges it somewhat in this way: David laughs. "What are you laughing at?" "Your head." "My head! what's the matter with my head?" "It looks like a cabbage." (It was in its exuberant state of release from the curl-papers.) Acres feels his head and says aside, "I am sorry I brought the fellow."

After a pause, he adds: "David, that will do," and out goes the honest dependent, laughing, to an effective exit. Acres then explains that David has been spoiled by the family in long service. The practice of the dance before the mirror is modified as to the text, and Sir Lucius O'Trigger is shown up as he is gliding about and bowing. An effect is gained. The original has it "a servant." Jefferson has it David, and in an aside he repeats his determination to send him back home, recovers his surprise and asks Sir Lucius: "How long have you been here?" The original text has it: "Acres—I send word of my arrival and receive answer that the lady is to be otherwise disposed of." Jefferson brings out the humor of his suit in idiomatic phrase with: "I send word that I am here, and the answer comes, 'You may go back'!" As to his rival, he adds: "I haven't seen him—and I don't believe anybody else has." "What's to be done?" says Sir Lucius. "It is to ask you that I sent for you," replies Acres. Thus motives and distinctness not technically clear in the original are provided at every point. When the point is not entirely clear it is repeated.

Long sentences are broken up and interrupted. "Does Company begin with a C or a K?" asks the original Bob Acres, and no further business is indicated. Jefferson haggles a little about the word, displays a slight distress, and finally leans over, whispers, and gets the response from O'Trigger of "with a C, of course." "Let the worst come of it, it will be off your mind tomorrow," is repeated by the anxious duellist. The bargaining for thirty-nine paces, if O'Trigger will not consent to forty or thirty-eight, is new. So is the jumping at the idea that O'Trigger will call out *his* man first.

The business and talk with David as to the letter of challenge that he holds in his hand are happily conceived.

These points, as others, grow directly out of the original, but are not expressed in it. "I warrant it smells of gunpowder," is the original suggestion by David. Jefferson adds: "Look out, David, it may go off!" He drops it, recovers himself with, "Whoever heard of a letter going off?" "David, hand me the letter." There is an admirable improvement in the scene where David gets on his knees in imploring terror and is ordered to stand up by the now well-frightened Bob. Among other new points are the joy and fresh confidence and swagger of Acres when Sir Lucius consults his watch and announces that the hour for the duel is past. Captain Absolute and Faulkland are seen coming. "They have no right to come now." "We won't run, I hope I won't run." "There will be little risk." "I don't care how little." How neatly is finish given to the part of David. In the closing scene he rushes in and carries off his master's pistol.

Mrs. Malaprop's mistake in giving to Captain Absolute the wrong letter—one addressed to her as the "Divine Delia"—is a comical addition. Her speech has a few new turns: "He is as graceful as a young gazette," "Patience on a mantelpiece," "circumscribe me," "conjunctions" instead of injunctions, "you go ahead, and I will precede you," etc.

Sir Anthony Absolute's joy at his son's enterprise in having written of Mrs. Malaprop as an "old harridan," and so on, is newly put. It would require great space to completely follow out this remarkable work of rearrangement and deft addition. What has been written must serve as a mere suggestion of the value that Mr. Jefferson's book of the play will possess in the days to come.

Dramatization is the result of technical skill applied to an existent romance or written material; and it ranges from work that is practically original to the merest hotchpotch. Some of it is scissoring only, and by a fortunate fluke may reach a success upon which to base false reputations. The methods of the novel and the drama differ widely, although some novelists write close to dramatic form. A playwright of genuine force breaks his material into pot-metal and recasts it. Such work is not unworthy. The plunderer with the scissors, elated with a success, often claims the drama as wholly his own, but the internal evidence puts him to shame infallibly with men who know dramatic processes. It is difficult to dramatize Dickens, for it is impossible to exclude his quaint genius, as paradoxically desirous as that may seem. It is the same difficulty that history presents in cases. Where the novelist is not familiar the drama may prevail. In any event, the drama must stand on its own merits and be complete in itself. It is as independent of its source as a child is of its parents after it reaches its majority. The critic or the public that relies upon the novel for information or pleasure at a performance, or the author who leaves any part of the play to this knowledge, is at fault. A drama is a drama by its own right, or it is nothing. It is a custom in France for an author to write the novel and then turn it into a drama.

Methods of adaptation may be observed by a comparison of the various stage editions of Shakspere's plays. See also such adaptations as that of Beaumont and Fletcher's "Maid's Tragedy," under the title of "The Bridal," by Sheridan Knowles and Macready.

Some of the dramas of Brougham, Boucicault, and Buckstone, compared with the originals, will show exquisite skill, while such a piece as "A Celebrated Case" is a model as a translation, or adaptation of language.

Innumerable dramatizations are easily accessible in the list of several thousand plays published by Samuel French. French writers are in the habit of dramatizing their own novels; the stage of the day furnishing constant examples of their methods.

Dumas first wrote "Camille" as a novel.

See "The Vicar of Wakefield," by Sterling Coyne. There is considerable variation in Will's dramatization of Goldsmith's story, as acted by Henry Irving, under the title of "Olivia." Dickens and Scott furnish abundant opportunities of comparison of the original novel with the dramatization.

Our own stage is pretty well burdened with things taken from foreign novels, without a bit of our bunting in them. There is hardly a particle of literary jute in them that has not been imported free of duty.

A leading manager has testified in court that "all plays at this time are adaptations and dramatizations." This is not altogether true. The expert can tell with certainty the genuineness of a play. The process of thought and construction in an honest play always gives warrant of the unborrowed play. It is almost impossible to deceive an observant critic in the matter. And, at any rate, the time has gone by when foreign plays can be stolen with lasting credit to the rogue.

CHAPTER IX.

FORMS OF THE DRAMA.

THE history of the drama furnishes many forms of construction, extinct as well as current, and as these proceed from the genius of the time allied with the genius of the individual writer, new forms more or less distinct will constantly appear. The drama has need to extend its territory. The recognized general rules of the drama, as herein discussed, maintain a certain authority in all of them; but each form has technical peculiarities. It is not within the scope of a book of general principles to more than indicate essential elements and differences. It is proper to suggest at this point that it is in the confusion of forms that moralists, managers, authors, actors, and critics, in their respective functions, not infrequently go astray in their judgment, action, and comment. The author of genuine taste will keep within the limits of the form he may have in hand, and not mix styles. Plays are, in kind, either artificial or natural, and embrace many varieties under the general divisions of tragedy and comedy.

Tragedy: The two great divisions of the drama are tragedy and comedy. The two share our life and possess our stage.

Tragedy is the drama of serious purport, where man is in conflict with his passions, with the chance of civil and social law, with the right and wrong of circumstance, in which passions, law, and circumstance are stronger than the individual. The Greek idea of destiny is practically an equivalent dramatic element. The chief peculiarity of tragedy is involved in the discussion of the conclusion of a play in Chapter III. Shakspere's tragedies provide an inevitable end for the hero; and wherever a version changing the result—as in the case of a happy ending to "Romeo and Juliet"—has been performed, failure has been the verdict. There is nothing in tragedy to avert the doom of Macbeth, of Hamlet, of Othello, and of Richard III.

Aristotle says that tragedy "effects through pity and terror the refinement of these and similar affections of the soul." There has been much surmise over the definition of "pity and terror";* but instinct and taste may be relied on to interpret the terms. In pure tragedy

* Aristotle.

mirth is unknown even in the most incidental passage. There is none of it in "Macbeth." The occasional scenes with fools and boors in Shakspere are imagined by some to indicate the necessity of dashes of humor in a play that concerns life and death. It is not so. There is no requirement in the law of contrast that a clown and a victim of destiny should be coupled.

It does not so happen in life as a rule. It may do so in a given case; then, let it. Even melodrama—as in "The Two Orphans"—does not always require comical incidents.

It is one of the dangers of mere technique that a false practice may prevail at times over technique based on principle. For example, again, should an author bring to a manager of to-day a tragedy in which all the causes and bearings have led to the legitimate ending, he may be confronted with the objection: "You have no love-interest in it!" Surely this is only a manager's decree. Surely there is no reason why every tragedy must have a love-sick maid in it, as if pure manhood had fled the world, and God had no hand in its affairs.

Is there room for a love-affair in "Macbeth"? Is Cordelia provided with a courtship under the moon in "Lear"? Does Richard III. waste his time in emotions of the heart? Does Cupid preside over the sessions of the conspirators in "Julius Cæsar"? Racine's "Athalie," the *chef-d'œuvre* of French tragedy, has no touch of love. No, no; each of these dramas has a theme. Guilty ambition, the ingratitude of children, the affairs of the State, and each theme in its own right occupies the drama. Love does largely enter into tragedy, perhaps abounds more than any other element, as we have warrant from all the list of dramas from "Romeo and Juliet" to "Venice Preserved" and "Adrienne" and countless more; but the subject, as cannot be too often said, controls the treatment. In historical themes in particular, the aim and purport is above and beyond the fond and trivial records of courtships. The feminine element is almost inseparable from any action; and the love of mother, wife, and daughter are not far to seek in the extremities of fate. It is not to be denied the managerial objection is sometimes correct in this matter, but by reason in the particular case. Thus Schiller was constrained to create Thecla in his "Wallenstein."

Comedy: Just as tragedy requires an inevitable but just and pitiful ending, so a comedy must have a happy conclusion. In a broad sense, then, "all that ends well" is comedy. In a strict sense, comedy is a play wherein a peaceful, orderly, diverting complication of purposes is agreeably disentangled. It is obvious that gloom has no place in it, and however excellent the play may be in all other respects, the purity of its comedy is impaired by a scene of death, a serious quarrel, or anything painful of the moment or in result. The killing of young Van Alstyne, practically by his father, in Mr. Bronson Howard's "Henrietta," is a case in point. It is a great comedy except for that. Tragedy is nature in a state of exaltation. Comedy is nature as we are familiar with it; something that any man at all acquainted with happiness has encountered, or may easily conceive. The moment the characters or incidents depart from nature, that moment pure comedy ceases, and burlesque or farce, or whatever it may be, begins. The English stage has what is known as the comedy of manners in "The School for Scandal," "The Rivals," "She Stoops to Conquer," etc., but, in truth, all pure comedy is comedy of manners. It is a truthful record of the times, or it falls into one of the artificial forms. The domestic comedy, the sentimental comedy, character comedy, comedy of intrigue, of conversation, and like classifications, are conveniently named because of the preponderance of certain elements. Schlegel is well worth consulting on comedy, and on the question of morality as concerned in it.

Artificial Comedy: Amusement being the object of comedy, we have the burlesque and the parody of other plays or scenes from them. The English burlesque in the hands of Planché reached great excellence, but its excessive punning in clumsy hands and the general downward tendency have degraded it. Its verses are usually clever. The characters borrowed largely from mythology fitted it to troops of dancing and sportive women. It is to be observed that consistency of character and the like are not important. Some of these lighter forms have much liberty in the acting by way of familiarity with the audience. Topical songs and allusions to matters of the day are even essential.

The farce, born in France, reached a successful point of cultivation in England, particularly under John Maddison Morton, who up to 1891 still lived to see its technique wholly unpracticed, if not lost. The farce was a thing of complications in one or two acts, and exaggerated nature just a trifle to gain effects. Much of the material left in this vast deposit has enriched the pieces of the latter-day thieves. Farce, like pure comedy in general, dependent on complications, requires no elaborate scenery. Simplicity in this technical point puts a long distance between it and the romantic. It is well to observe here that each form of the drama has some such mark of distinction in usage.

Negro Minstrelsy: A native form of drama in the United States is negro minstrelsy, the merry comedy of negro life. It has now about passed away under the stress of sentimental ballads and costumes of silk and satin. See Hutton's "Curiosities of the American Stage."

Farce Comedy: An American product that has sprung up since about 1870 is the farce comedy, improperly so called, for it lacks the sharp consistency of farce and the essential naturalness of comedy. It is significant that it has no honest name. It is a conglomerate of acted anecdotes, odd sayings, burlesqueries and grotesqueries, gathered from all quarters.

Those that succeed best have a faint outline of a story. They harbor immature young women in short skirts, abound in song and dance, and could not exist without the special doings of quaint actors. The concoctions of Hoyt have bits of genuine humor; and the class, trivial as it is, opposed to orderly art as it is, must be accepted as indicative of American genius. It may be curious to read after a while that it was accounted comical and an original bit of humor, to leave, by means of a mechanical arrangement, a hatchet sticking in the head of an enemy, or a friend for that matter, as it makes no difference in this kind of comedy. In like manner you crack a walnut on the head of a casual acquaintance and a bump appears. There is no telling what comical exaggeration will be encountered. Does not Dr. Mulo Medicus emerge from the hot spring with green hair? In "The Bunch of Keys" the clerk conveniently lights a match by scraping it on the bald head of a guest as he registers his name. In Dixey's "Adonis" an organ-grinder's monkey wears a bell-punch to register his collections. Dixey's piece held the constant attention of New York for about three years, and challenged the amazement and amusement of the British. Adonis is a statue endowed with life, and until he is recalled to his pedestal his time is devoted to escaping from a female purchaser. He permits the villain to disarm him, and to press against his breast with the foil might and main. "Oh, it won't hurt me! My breast-bone is of marble." He imitates Irving as Richard III., coming on as a milkman with a can, and diverts his audience at the pump. Engaged as a clerk at a country store, he assumes a new disguise for each customer. One visitor, Bunion Turke, he shaves, the cup used by the barber being attached by an elastic string to the wall, and is made to play about the customer's head in a lively fashion. Bunion must move his head back and forth to accommodate the brush held rigid. Bunion wears a tremendous diamond on his bosom when he enters, and Adonis sweeps it off and pockets it with great presence of mind. Adonis telephones for a glass of beer, and a moment later opens the box and gets it. Dixey does many absurd things, and is in the main diverting; while the other characters, among which is a mechanical mule, with a dangerous leg and the semblance of a hog, to which as it wanders on Bunion Turke addresses his always unfinished plaint, "Te-went-y years ago." This is farce-comedy. It knows but one law—comicality.

In Moser's plays an idea or sentiment is played with, used for mechanism, and not seized upon as a genuine thing. Moser abandons the theme—as all farce-comedies do—or lets leading characters drop and brings forward subordinate ones.

Spectacular pieces are a mixture of all the elements that give opportunity for the display of the human form, with dancing, processions, masses, scenic and musical effects. By nature they are romantic or melodramatic, fantastic and allegorical, derived from fable or story, drawn from remote times and lands.

The opera is a drama of slight but often concentrated texture, in which the emotions are largely interpreted by music.

It invites absurdities that are taken seriously, for song in life is an absurd means of discourse to begin with; but it all illustrates how far the imagination will go in reconciling the improbable and the impossible with the necessities of a stage and the technique of any form of the drama. Breadth of treatment is its rule. Scribe's librettos * are models. It is largely spectacular in nature, and the lighter forms of opera, requiring ballets, color in costume, etc., are generally based on material not too close to our daily life.

The vaudeville is more practical. Song and dance are old adjuncts to the lighter forms of the drama.

The pantomime and the ballet are usually combined. The pantomime is drama in mute performance, and consequently limited in effects. On the Continent it is a distinguished branch of art, and the dancing of the ballet has innumerable expressive forms.

* Librettos by Scribe.

The Offenbach opera. The light-hearted genius of Paris composed a new style of opera for the general merriment of the world. Who can describe the surprises, the quaintness of song, the drolleries of action of the Offenbach school? It was the intoxicating wine of music. Gladstone, when premier of England, found time to say that the world owed as much in its civilization to the discovery of the fiddle as it did to steam.

This cannot be applied in its whole sense to Offenbach, but this master of satire and the sensuous certainly expressed his times. He set laughter to song. It was democratic. It spared not king, courtier, or the rabble. It was wisdom and sentiment in disguise. It was born among despotisms, and jested when kingdoms fell. It was the stalking horse behind which Offenbach hunted the follies of the day and bagged the absurdities of the hour. If it had *double entendre*, its existence had a double meaning. Its music and purpose defied national prejudices. Under its laughter-compelling notes the sober bass-viol put on a merry disposition, and your cornet-a-piston became a wag. It was flippant, the glorification of youthful mirth and feelings, and it made many a melancholy Jacques sing again the song of Béranger,

"*Comme je regrette ma jambe si dodu.*"

It is not the purpose here to commend its delirious dances, but to admit that there was genius in it. In a technical sense the dramatic part of them are models compared with the inane and vague compositions of a later school.

The opera bouffe is in a stage beyond decadence, and no longer regards consistency, even of nonsense, in its dramatic elements. Some of the conventionalisms of its technique remain.

We hear again and again the old choruses, the drinking songs, the letter songs, the wine songs, the conspirators' songs, the departure for the war, the lovers' duets, and what-not, with the old goblets, the old helmets and all in use; but order is lost, and the topical song often saves the public patience, apart from the *disjecta membra*, upon which are fed the eye and the ear.

The Gilbert opera. The delicate foolery of Gilbert and the interpreting melody of Sullivan created an inimitable form of opera that delighted its generation. In its way perfection marks it. There is much in it that ministers to inward quiet and enjoyment. "Pinafore," "The Mikado," and all the list, are products of genius. "Ruddygore" is structurally weak, proving that even nonsense must have a logical treatment. Successful in a manner as "Ruddygore" was, it was filled with characteristic quaintness. We accept Rose Maybud as a piece of good luck, from the moment her modest slippers demurely patter to the front; and it is a sober statement to say that our generation has seen nothing more charming than her artful artlessness and innocence. She is worthy of Gilbert. His taste is refined beyond the point of vulgarity in essence or by way of expediency. His fancy is not tainted with the corruption of flesh-tight limbs, and he holds fast only to such physical allurements as the "three little maids just from school" in the "Mikado" or the impossibly good and dainty Rose Maybud may tempt us with. In the dance there is no lasciviousness, only joy. Gilbert and Sullivan have called a halt to the can-can and bid the world be decent. The whole history of comic opera is filled with proof that music first consented to lend itself to foolery on condition that there should be some heart in it; and even Offenbach, the patriarch of libidinous absurdities, could not get along without stopping by the wayside to make his sinners sing love-songs filled with pure emotion.

Rose Maybud is a piece of delicate coquetry with the mysterious simplicity of maidenhood, giving offense in no way. These authors are satirists, not burlesquers and fakirs.

The historical play. A dignified and worthy branch of the dramatic art is the historical play. The mere reproduction of archæology is not dramatic, for it is only the human that is so. The historical is beset with difficulties. The drama cannot safely and honestly controvert history, and the chosen material must be pretty much complete in itself. In an invented story, not historical in nature, the author can exclude all disturbing preconceptions. The historical character is usually too diffuse. The incidents and scope of a career extend beyond the dramatist's canvas. Where the life has one dramatic moment, with which the popular mind alone concerns itself, the dramatist has a perfect property. Thus Queen Mary, Joan of Arc, Charlotte Corday, Mary Antoinette, old John Brown, William Tell, and scores of others, are apt subjects. It would be difficult, on the other hand, to make anything out of Frederick the Great, or the great Napoleon. Incidents in their lives may furnish plays, but these must be sketchy and fragmentary. After the lapse of time the public vision narrows, and Abraham Lincoln liberating the slaves may admit of a romance and action. It is, however, not the lapse of time only. The principle is unity of purpose and deed in that life and the absence of controverting general knowledge. The invented story may be as true history as anything in the record. One can't make a comedy figure out of Marie Antoinette—it has been tried—or of Mary Stuart. The historical idea will have its own. It does not matter how important or interesting characters or events are historically, if not dramatic in incident, length, and breadth, they are not suited for a play.

The romantic drama. The drama of Shakspere and his circle is Gothic in structure as compared with the classic forms of the French stage. They are also essentially romantic. Remoteness of time or country is, to a great extent, essential. Possibilities become realities, and we do not set up a close rule of probability.

Romantic plays by preference are verse; but the language of the Elizabethan poets is lost. The music in Shakspere is constitutional. A book on blank verse is extant. The writers of the school of Sheridan Knowles fell into a technical requirement that is peculiar to them—opportunities for declamation, such as the description of the hunt by Constance in "The Love Chase," passages in "The Wife," etc. There is a good deal of poetic nonsense in all of them, such as in "The Lady of Lyons," where we find the expressions "a spirit of bloom" and "the shadow of the dear starlight of thy haunting eyes." "The Honeymoon" is full of it. This form of verse holds to "thee" and "thou" and all manner of archaisms.

Much that bears on the romantic play is treated under the head of the probable. We have the truly romantic, as in Shakspere, and the pseudo-romantic, as in "Ruy Blas," and lesser things.

In the main the purpose is to sow spiritual things. The romantic is an element that has its place. The plays built of air-castles get us away from the realities of life.

The melodrama, with greater breadth of treatment and insistence on situation, is closely related to the romantic. Custom has made the admixture of humor a technical requirement. This marks a strong distinction between it and tragedy. Melodrama keeps pace with the life of the day and is a durable form. The story, appealing largely to the imagination, often jumps safely over much detail.

There is not much good healthy English melodrama. The soil is deep, but the harvest is poor in quality. The tendency is to be brutal in order to make a theatrical point. The author of "The Wages of Sin," "Ring of Iron," and "Woman against Woman," with the brawn of a blacksmith forges strong plays of the sort. Unmerciful he is to a degree. See how he puts his boot-heel on virtue, and note how he lets the flickering tongue of scandal do its fatal work. He seems to be an imperfect nature, writing with an iron hand, like some literary Goetz von Berlichingen. He is a dragon of unpleasant truths.

In "Woman against Woman," a wife is suspected of being the mother of a child not born in the neighborhood of the statute, but really the incorporation of the moral views of her sister. The sister is married to a lord, and to protect her—unworthy in every way—the heroine sticks to a lie at the expense of her own happiness and that of every other person. These are hot plowshares of brutality.

Melodrama, while often romantic, is usually of coarser texture than the romantic proper, and always involves deadly peril in its critical situations, which are suggested and emphasized by a certain touch of music—*melos*, the Greek word for music, furnishing the first part of the compound name. It is the semi-tragedy of life.

The best type of the melodrama is furnished by the French stage. If "Lagardere" were considered with reference to the crime in it— if one should imagine that the strictures on the story of Gwynne in Chapter II. are based on the fallacy that "crime" is not fit dramatic material —it should be condemned with tenfold the vehemence. It is, on the contrary, filled with ten delightful murders; two weaklings are spared by virtue of their cowardice, and perhaps one or two more killings were judicious. But our homes are not touched in the play of Bourgeois and Féval. We accept the story laid in the romantic days of the year 1700.

The element of suspense is wonderfully illustrated in this drama of action, that leaps from its prologue to its first act over a lapse of sixteen years without a boggle; that traverses mountains, fights in moats, and gets its hero into close quarters in his enemy's lodgings, and lets him out triumphantly by lifting a drop and converting the scene into the ante-chamber of the Prince Regent. Sympathize with "Lagardere"? If played right you do, but the actors all must know, as it were, the secret thrust of Lagardere. The movement must be so quick that we ask nothing of the probabilities. It must be like the flaming sword of the Sergeant in "Far from the Madding Crowd," or the battle-ax of Umslopogaas. We see the effect. "Lagardere" is the work of an "impressionist." It must be presented at the right point of view.

The production needs slashing quickness of action.

It could be easily demonstrated by an analysis of the play that its magic lies in the way it is acted. Slow work is fatal. In reading it, one ponders in vain to make out the coherency. It violates all common rules. Perhaps the receptive processes of the generation are slower than they were when the romantic drama flourished. Yet how readily we accept the reasonableness of the Duchess de Nevers remaining a recluse in her chamber for seventeen years. How quickly we forget the contradiction of purpose in Gonzague, who is seeking for a false daughter in the place of the lost Blanche, where it is to his interest not to find her—and yet he is seeking her. In a few weeks her husband, the Duke de Gonzague, is empowered to call together a family council, and if by then the child is not found, "the estate passes to the mother, and through her to him." But somehow we accept it all. We watch the thrust of Lagardere's blade with a thrilling God-speed. Why? Because we accept the romantic premises. We enlist—we volunteer—with Lagardere for the war. It is a question of theatrical illusion, and not of morals or taste. There is a volume in the distinction. We had a starting-point of interest in " Lagardere." We had none in the story of Gwynne.

A curious error is the belief, sometimes encountered, that romanticism and complication of plot are the same things. On the contrary, such stories as " Paul and Virginia," " Picciola," that have stirred the world, are exceedingly simple. The romantic is usually remote from common life. In Germany the negro in his savage state is a favorite theme for poetry, etc.

Mere romance as material is misleading, for very commonplace people have romantic lives, or a series of romantic events to happen to them, as in " Arabian Nights." The romance in a drama must be inherent and not accidental.

To this muster of the forms of the drama very many other classifications might be added, the foreign stage abounding in distinctions, but chiefly the purpose has been to make clear that the character of a play is determined by the preponderance of some one or more elements. The theme dictates its own terms as to tone, spirit, and proportions, while all may be freely adapted to the general laws of dramatic construction. Reference to the best examples of the various classes accessible in published form will enable the student to better arrive at their characteristic distinctions.

Even in the same forms there may be differences of treatment; consequently, one should read a manuscript play worthy of attention many times before judgment. It depends on *where* the power lies. It may be in a character—accomplished by breadth—simplicity in the story and detail in the treatment. So that very often the better the play the less you understand its technical values at a reading.

There are character plays and plays of plot; subjective and objective plays; plays for the eye, the ear, and emotion, laughter; physiological, ideal, and realistic plays, etc., and finally —chaos.

It is best to write for the times. It would be well if we had a repertory theatre, but neither London nor New York has. New York, in particular, no longer revives plays from the dead. Everything is for the moment. Art might fare better if the stock-company system and some regard for the old and the newly classic prevailed. But lacking them, the constant cry is for newness.

CHAPTER X.

CRITICISM.

THE critical temperament is kindly and forgiving; it exalts the true, kindles the fire of timid hearts in capable breasts, and is only fierce in words of dispraise where presumptuous imbecility uses a false authority to mislead. It pities stupidity, and punishes it as a crime only when it becomes a danger. Having all the warmth of a writer who is all disproportion, the one with the critical temperament has the judicial mind that gives value to praise and weight to censure. It is no part of its duty always to add to the discomforts of artistic failure and the loss of managerial money by dwelling on obvious incompetency in production or stupidity in matters of judgment. It withholds the easy jest, and the good word of cheer is oftener spoken than the dispraise that would serve no just purpose; but it stands between the players and the public, and its duty to that public sometimes demands plainer speaking than is agreeable to those in the responsible charge of furnishing the entertainment that is such a material part of modern life. There is this peculiarity incident to all criticism, that genuine feeling cannot be simulated; and the rudest pen manifests grace when the heart simply tells what it has in turn been told. The truest words have been written about the greatest actors, where the critic was content to be but the reporter. Thus, technical knowledge is not wholly the best requisite, and all that a manager and the public can ask from the competent critic anywhere is sincerity. Let him not be warped by his learning, nor turned aside by the influences within and around him.

When Charles Lamb wrote of Mrs. Jordan's Viola, he not only contributed to our knowledge and our perfect understanding perhaps the most striking picture of an actress in all the literature of the stage, but he gave to us that passage in his writings that most commends him to our hearts. The gentle Elia said: "Those who have only seen Mrs. Jordan within the last ten or fifteen years can have no adequate notion of her performances of such parts as Ophelia, Helena, in 'All's Well That Ends Well,' and Viola in this play. Her voice had lately acquired a coarseness which suited well enough with her Nells and hoidens, but in those days it sank, with her steady and melting eye, into the heart. Her joyous parts—in which her memory now chiefly lives—in her youth were outdone by her plaintive ones. There is no giving an account how she delivered the disguised story of her love for Orsino. She used no rhetoric in her passion; or, it was nature's own rhetoric, most legitimate then when it seemed altogether without rule or law."

There is in this exquisite sentence of true criticism the music of truth. Somehow, no man knows, it contains all the plaintive sweetness of the hidden love, revealed to the hapless actress, who had the inner vision of Shakspere's meaning.

This is the critical temperament in its best illustration. Hazlitt had the same faculty. The race of great actors obtained full response from men with that fine instinct that makes the critic, rather than mere knowledge. Even when he goes astray the receptive critic has a merit unknown to the arbiters who disdain sentiment, as if it were a corrupter of the mind and false to analysis.

The individual theatre-goer loves an honest criticism, and as criticisms are widely read, the word of disapprobation for stupidity or falseness of any kind in the art or in the intent are sure to go home to an appreciative reader. Of all writers for the press, a critic does not preach in the wilderness. The theatre-goer loves to be strengthened in correct views, and likes the explanation of doubts that rise in his own mind, and wishes to have shown to him why he revolted against this and that.

Criticism is absolutely essential to public morals and public taste. It is a guide to the people and a protector of the realm. Its responsibilities really require as high character and as strong force as the staff of a newspaper possesses. It is an honorable service, and a life like that of William Winter, devoted to the work of criticism, will be rewarded with a memory not inferior to that of Hazlitt or Lamb. His writing has been more voluminous and more exacting than theirs.

Others of the period of William Winter have record of distinction; but an important part of Winter's work has found its way into book form, and thus belongs to the permanent literature of the stage. In England Clement Scott and others, as members of that higher court that determines all merit, exercise their functions worthily; while Jules Le Maitre, Francesque Sarcey, and others in France sustain art in its purity.

In point of fact, the managers could not exist without the very frankness of comment which so often calls them back to reason. They would be bankrupt in a season or two without this wholesome correction. The truth about a play is what should be told at all times. It is true that a criticism, unless far more exhaustive than time usually permits immediately after a first performance, can only be a statement of a part of the case. A criticism, then, should aim at proportion within limits. Its qualifications should be distinct. It should not mislead either by censure or praise. The seat of criticism is naturally at the centre of dramatic art; as London, Paris, New York; and there it has peculiar difficulties, such as arise, for example, from the associations of club life, operative in various ways, and a certain provincialism of likes and dislikes. It is a newspaper instinct and the critic's duty to be true to the public. It is no part of this book to attempt universal instruction in these matters. It essays only comment on the value of the work and certain qualities that obviously belong to the exercise of its power.

Criticism is at fault that searches out minor faults. Such things belong to the limitations of art, and are to be discussed in the workshop. The matter that concerns the public is the sum of all the impressions—that which it carries away as a reminiscence, and not a possibly unavoidable technical defect that it would not see unless it were pointed out.

Where a fault is worthy of attention censure should be sustained by proof—otherwise it is discredited often enough by the reader, and always by the actor. The well-trained critic knows his theme as well as the actor knows his business, and it is a common experience with him to have his comments treated as an impertinence. In the plays of Shakspere this is particularly true. Your man of the stage persuades himself that he has gained a peculiar franchise in producing a piece that is common property. Yet Shakspere requires the highest measure of criticism.

Every play should be criticised after its kind, and every actor after his style. It should be observed that there is a vast difference between manner and mannerism. There is an end of all just criticism and of all progression and freedom in art where fixity of manner is insisted upon. An idea should be expressed in the way fittest for the actor. That he may be unsuited to a part is also true. This does not preclude an actor of genius from following tradition in the main in some given performance.

It is an error for manager and actor to take refuge against criticism in believing that it is only one man's opinion. It is usually the world's opinion; and if it is not, the disproof is at hand. All criticism may be wrong in a given case, but it will be an accident. There is abundant false judgment, for that matter. Perhaps the greatest danger to good judgment is the fact that a centre of art, being at the van, too quickly lays aside old forms. If Sardou is in power at the leading theatres, work not on his model is not sufficiently regarded. There are so many kinds of dramas, old and new, that the latest techniques should not be subversive of all else that is good. Moreover, the best function of criticism is not in finding fault, but in upholding the good.

Hypercriticism is an odious evil. Art has so much to contend against in America, lack of subvention and the rareness of the stock system, that it is hard indeed for it to have to silently suffer critical falsities; and unnecessary criticism is as bad as the untrue. Hypercriticism could busy itself with Shakspere. Benedix, the German dramatist, wrote a book against him.

The amount of criticism to be given to a play should not depend upon the "importance" of the piece. The play may be a dire failure, and "beneath criticism" for the writer who is not moved to do his full duty to the public. In fact, opportunity for the most useful critical work may be furnished by a play of no moment.

One of the most uncertain elements to be encountered on the road by a theatrical manager is the manner of his reception by the press, particularly of the smaller but growing and ambitious towns, where dramatic criticism is undergoing the process of development. It is a curious condition of affairs, but regarded from a business point of view it is not without its compensations. The fortunate circumstance that there is no uniformity of journalistic judgment sustains the weaklings of the profession. If the stuffed club of criticism were laid with unerring justice on every back that invited blows, many a Thespian, deserving enough personally, would hunger more than he does, and many a wretched combination would experience tragedy in its real form. It is a strange confusion on all sides. The unknowingness or the charity of the critic is met by the most persistent self-esteem of the actor. The life of the player is at best one of delusions, where the chief delight is flattery. No actor can be so poor in his art, no manager so thoroughly convinced of the inferiority of his attraction, as to accept truth from a critic " on the road." Criticism is not regarded as the proper function of the rural press. And yet this press may be the very one that hits the nail on the head, when it has been missed all along. Truth is truth wherever we find it. It is a healthful irregularity. At times your embryo critic is fierce, at times wild. The road has already got to be hedged with the tangle-brier of this flowering variety. The critic in a state of development has the capricious nature of a maiden when she begins to wear her crown and to feel her power when she is first sought. His virtue is something that admits of no smile from the advance agent, that bold, bad man of sin. He feels a keen rivalry with the critic around the corner, and generally knows what view will be advanced by that perverted individual.

His public expects from him a degree of rhetorical flourish that is best adapted to praise, and to this he is prone; but his wrath may fall on the right spot in due season. It is a delight to see the Eastern success that has escaped censure by some accident fall a prey to these young gentlemen of the West with moral sentiments and correct tastes. The true function of the reviewer of a public performance, in addition to the exercise of artistic perceptions, united with a knowledge of some system of intelligent analysis, is to produce the effect experienced by an audience. Criticism, in the sense of serious discussion, for example, is not possible as to the best types of opera-bouffe—a species of entertainment that concerns the eye and the ear, a form of amusement that brings us into personal relations for the moment with certain absurd figures of the stage. Its pre-eminent quality is folly, and this we must not confront with wisdom. The naïve and generous pen of the Western critic is true to the best methods when it gracefully enters into descriptive writing. It is the genuine temperament subject to the impressions of the moment.

He and his public have the courage of their likings, and the generous confession of admiration for the ballet girl in blue tricot is not less creditable than the execration of the misfits that by some strange fatality accompany high art, and that used to be seen in heavy and pretentious operas.

We need enthusiasm, and the critic should foster it. The public is not afraid of sentiment, and the critic should not be. The public has the courage of its likings, and where grace, melody, sentiment, sincerity, or what-not carries it, "criticism" is the emptiest of vocations. Surely the public may err at times, but that is another matter. Sentiment is the object of the drama, and a critic has no right to be impassive.

This reference to criticism in the large and small towns apart from the metropolis, is to emphasize the fact that there sometimes the most valuable criticism may be found. It applies to England or any other country, but in particular to America, where centres of population are increasing, and where critics of experience and of genius for their task may be found.

In point of fact the critic should be a specialist and be permanent in his position—one of the best and most entertaining writers on the staff. With the right men in the right place, the verdict of one town will not be reversed by the verdict of another, except on principle.

There are few perfect plays in a technical sense; and even the best are refracted by time.

It is entirely unprofitable to split hairs about scenes that one has witnessed better done. Leave that to the old men who swear by the authority of their shrunken hams, and who are testy on the subject of Julia Dean, Ellen Tree, and Mrs. Mowatt. True criticism is concerned with first principles all the time.

A like spurious criticism is the substitution of historical data in the place of present comment. When a thing was done at the old Bowery or the Winter Garden or Drury Lane has nothing to do with the merits of the case.

The range of criticism is as broad as life—only it is not necessary to criticise everything. Perfunctory words are an evil also. In a republic, where the State does nothing for the stage, the helpful offices of the newspaper critic are of vast importance.

CHAPTER XI.

HOW A DRAMA IS BUILT UP.—ADVICE TO THE DRAMATIST.

In seeking to be useful to the dramatic writer, there is some temptation at this point to devote the space to an analysis of some familiar drama, giving the application of the principles of art involved in its building; but it would require a volume to do this in anything like a complete manner, and when done it would in many of its details concern but one of the many forms of the drama. Once familiar with the principles, the play-writer can use them. Let him accept them fully and without compromise, and by the strength of the faith that is in him he will soon proceed to exercise these principles in good works.

The dramatic principles stated in this book are not formidable, and care has been taken not to give them a complicated look by a multitude of numbered rules and subdivisions; but the writer, by much repetition, all proper enough in its place, has sought to prefer with earnestness the conception that play-writing is above all a matter of common sense. Managers receive plays without end from all kinds of people—from the school-girl to the judge on the bench. One would think that they imagine a play to be something entirely apart from human possibilities; something in which the language is to be exceedingly vulgar or exceedingly fine —finer than ever Jove spake.

How a writer acquires an aptitude for any form of writing it is not always easy to determine. Circumstances have much to do with it, and the inner springs of his nature have more. The elements of any form of writing may be taught. There can be no question of that. The simplest school rhetoric will lay the foundation for a style that will charm mankind. The one who is to write the leaders in the newspapers that are to control public opinion, or who is to clothe sentiment in a way to touch the general heart in his books, is now learning at the schools how to stake out a composition. If the boy can be taught to write a composition, the man can be "taught to write a play." Playwriting is a species of composition, and it is entirely proper for any disciple of literature to essay its principles; and it is no reflection upon the genuine powers of his mind if he discovers that his aptitude does not lie in that quarter.

Does the young author realize the significance of a successful play? Does he reflect that it must be submitted first to readers and managers who are familiar with the strictest requirements of art, and that finally, if it reaches the great public, it must encounter the common sense and the common sentiment of the world? It would seem not. You may be sure that you cannot hide a defect so deep that it will not rise up against you. You may be sure that the weak point that you were dimly conscious of the child may cry out against in the acting, and that any variation from common sense and common morality, or whatever else the fault may be, will be discovered. It is a bright light that beats on the stage.

As a rule, the amateur writer may be sure that his subject has been better treated by some other writer, and that the manager can put his hand on a score of plays with substantially the same situations.

The student of principle will gain many new aspects of principle if he will seek for himself in plays illustrations of what is set forth in this book. Let him analyze Shakspere, or take up anything in print, good or bad. There is nothing more instructive than a cheap but effective conventional melodrama. By this large acquaintance with plays one also learns the distinctions between the forms. These distinctions, being mainly conventional and not broad enough to supplant general principles stated in this book, are essential. The number of acts for a farce, the number of songs to a play that will make either an opera or a vaudeville out of it, and the like, must be ascertained by the special study indicated. The principles are modified but never destroyed by these variations in the application of them.

The mental process of evolving a drama out of given material could never be the same with any two authors. The philosophy of the theme and the principles of construction might be identical. Every true play fashioned under a creative hand has its germ. This germ may be a pregnant and suggestive trait in some character, a happening; of personal knowledge in life, an incident in history, a paragraph in a newspaper —in short, a dramatic idea from any source. Charles Reade admittedly sought with diligence the history of each day as the press abundantly gathered its comedies and tragedies. It was a newspaper paragraph casually read that set Schiller's genius at work on "Cabale und

Liebe." This germ of a play is no slight matter. If it be a situation, climacteric or terminal, the mind works back to the causes. If it be a cause, the evolution proceeds to the logical result. The way is not always direct or the means always clear. Months of patient thought and a further time of patient work may be between conception and completion. A period of gestation is required. If the thoughts that come and go in this time were set down—the tentative things, the temptations, the mistakes, the vagaries, and all the mass of non-essential or superfluous material rejected for the needful and the true—it would teach the unskilled that play-writing is something more than a trick. The dramatic idea requires a knowledge of all its possibilities and surroundings as the first condition. If the play is to concern itself with high society, or the slums, or the sailor ashore, or anarchy, or war, or the money-exchange, or what-not—that subject is to be mastered. It may happen that you are thoroughly informed in the matter. It may be involved in your life. If so, so much the better. Your pen will journey along with speed in proportion with your familiarity with the subject. The drama then comes by way of distillation, drop by drop; accidental things fall away, and out of the rude block the form begins to appear. The process of selection and rejection does not end with the manuscript. The weighing of every grain is not enough, the sum total must correspond; and it requires an unerring mind to have a perfect balance before a piece is given to the public. Careful dress rehearsals may do it. The rehearsal is part of the authorship, and there he will find a new Alp to climb. In fact, some plays, as is the history of " Hazel Kirke," are not completed until public opinion has been brought to bear on the performances.

We have seen that the dramatic idea may be suggested by an accidental revelation of this, that, or the other part of it. In like manner the actual technical work may begin at any part. An author may conceive a scene in all of its true proportions and commit it to paper, leaving untouched his chief situations; but at this stage the outline of the drama exists in the poet's mind. If, by way of comparison, a painter is clear in mind and sure in hand, he may not even trace with crayon the lines of proportion on his canvas. He may begin at the nose or the eye. The principles are the same. And so the dramatist may choose his own way; but one distinction the untried author must always bear in mind: A play is not written, it is constructed.

This is true primarily even of the drama in verse.

Writing is dangerously fluent because it is subjective. Dramatic speech is the expression of an author's research into the minds of others. The mental process of the dramatist is not necessarily hesitating at all points, but the unskilled manipulator of dramatic material must reconcile himself to self-denial and delays in composition.

Wilkie Collins is in such large measure dramatic in his novels that his own account of his processes of thought in producing his novels will illustrate what has been herein suggested. He wrote in 1887:

" My first proceeding is to get my central idea—the pivot on which the story turns. The central idea of ' The Woman in White ' is the idea of a conspiracy in private life, in which circumstances are so handled as to rob a woman of her identity by confounding her with another woman sufficiently like her in personal appearance to answer the wicked purpose. The destruction of her identity represents a first division of the story; the recovery of her identity marks a second division. My central idea next suggests some of my chief characters.

" A clever devil must conduct the conspiracy.

Male devil or female devil? The sort of wickedness wanted seems to be a man's wickedness. Perhaps a foreign man. Count Fosco faintly shows himself to me before I know his name.

"I let him wait, and begin to think about the two women. They must be both innocent and both interesting. Lady Glyde dawns on me as one of the innocent victims. I try to discover the other—and fail. I try what a walk will do for me—and fail. I devote the evening to a new effort—and fail. Experience tells me to take no more trouble about it, and leave that other woman to come of her own accord. The next morning, before I have been awake in my bed for more than ten minutes, my perverse brains set to work without consulting me. Poor Anne Catherick comes into the room and says, 'Try me.'

"I have got an idea; I have got three of my characters. What is there to do now? My next proceeding is to begin building up the story. Here my favorite three efforts must be encountered. First effort: to begin at the beginning. Second effort: to keep the story always advancing without paying the smallest attention to the serial division in parts, or to the book publications in volumes. Third effort: to decide on the end. All this is done, as my father used to paint his skies in his famous sea-pieces, at one heat. As yet I do not enter into details; I merely set up my landmarks. In doing this the main situations of the story present themselves in all sorts of new aspects. These discoveries lead me nearer and nearer to finding the right end. The end being decided on, I go back again to the beginning, and look at it with a new eye, and fail to be satisfied with it. I have yielded to the worst temptation that besets a novelist—the temptation to begin with a striking incident, without counting the cost in the shape of explanations that must and will follow. These pests of fiction to reader and writer alike can only be eradicated in one way. I have already mentioned the way—to begin at the beginning. In the case of 'The Woman in White' I get back, as I vainly believe, to the true starting-point of the story. I am now at liberty to set the new novel going, having, let me repeat, no more than an outline of story and characters before me, and leaving the details in each case to the spur of the moment. For a week, as well as I can remember, I work for the best part of every day, but not as happily as usual. An unpleasant sense of something wrong worries me. At the beginning of the second week a disheartening discovery reveals itself. I have not found the right beginning of 'The Woman in White' yet. The scene of my opening chapters is in Cumberland. Miss Fairlie (afterward Lady Glyde); Mr. Fairlie, with his irritable nerves and his art treasures; Miss Halcombe (discovered suddenly, like Anne Catherick), are all waiting the arrival of the young drawing-master, Walter ·Hartright. No; this won't do. The person to be first introduced is Anne Catherick. She must already be a familiar figure to the reader when the reader accompanies me to Cumberland. This is what must be done, but I don't see how to do it; no new idea comes to me; I and my manuscript have quarreled and don't speak to each other. One evening I happen to read of a lunatic who has escaped from an asylum—a paragraph of a few lines only in a newspaper. Instantly the idea comes to me of Walter Hartright's midnight meeting with Anne Catherick, escaped from the asylum. 'The Woman in White' begins again, and nobody will ever be half as much interested in it now as I am. From that moment I have done with my miseries. For the next six months the pen goes on. It is work, hard work, but the harder the better, for this excellent reason: the work is its own exceeding great reward. As an example of the gradual manner in which I reached the development of character, I may return for a moment to Fosco. The making him fat was an afterthought; his canaries and his white mice were found next; and the most valuable discovery of all, his admiration of Miss Halcombe, took its rise in a conviction that he would not be true to nature unless there was some weak point somewhere in his character."

Concerning his own manner of working, Ibsen says:

"When I am writing, I must be alone; if I have eight characters of a drama to do with I have society enough; they keep me busy; I must learn to know them. And this process of making their acquaintance is slow and painful. I make, as a rule, three casts of my dramas, which differ considerably from each other. I mean in characteristics, not in the course of the treatment. When I first settle down to work out my material, I feel as if I had got to know my characters on a railway journey; the first acquaintance is struck up, and we have chatted about this and that. When I write it down again, I already see everything much more clearly, and I know the people as if I had stayed with them for a month at a watering-place. I have grasped the leading points of their characters and their little peculiarities, but I might yet make a mistake in important points. At last, in the final cast, I have reached the limits of my acquaintance; I know my people from close and lasting intercourse; they are my trusted friends, who have no surprises in store for me; as I see them now, so shall I always see them."

The chief figures in a play appear at once in the action as it is revolved in the mind. Contrast suggests the character or characters in opposition. Certain situations and incidents can only be brought about by the contributing influence of others, and thus a character has to be created that was not at all in the first scheme. This new-comer may be needed for the sake of variety, or to supply some element more or less closely related to the main movement.

It is hard to change what is once written. The painter who once gets a leg out of position may never get it right. The sculptor is in a worse case. If he chips too deep his material is ruined. Thus material things must first be determined.

It has been urged that an author should be an actor. This claim that no man should be free of the guild except that he tread the stage, is specious, but false. The art of writing a play and the art of acting a part are distinct.

One should know the stage, but he must know nature first, and have it in mind above all things. Shakspere and Molière, men of extraordinary genius, were actors by coincidence, and were not distinguished in that capacity. The coincidence does not exist in large proportion in that long list of writers of the Elizabethan period. The conspicuous authors of this day—Dumas, Sardou, Bronson Howard, Henry Arthur Jones, W. S. Gilbert, and others—do not sustain any such assumed rule. The limitations of the stage may be learned without acting. Lessing and Schiller and Goethe did not have to get their genius from Thespians. In fact, the dramatist will always find that he has the rights of the drama to maintain against the imperfect views and self-interest of actors. The principles of construction and of dramatic effect determine the things of the stage, and no single class of men.

This may be said in friendly warning to the young author: the manager of a theatre and the director of his stage are, or are presumed to be, skilled in their business. The manager, as a man of business, has his policy of management. He knows what kind of plays he is willing to back with his capital and his resources. He has employed his company and equipped his house accordingly. It is not to the purpose to besiege a manager with a drama that he cannot possibly use. The manager and the director of the stage understand theatrical effects, and their suggestions should have value; but here again no personal authority can be superior to correct principles.

The dramatic instinct is essential in addition to a knowledge of technique. One may have genius in some other line, like Richelieu in statesmanship, and yet lack the dramatic faculty. On the other hand, a man of no literary turn may instinctively know how to set his dramatic squadron in the field. The reason, no doubt, why so many distinguished poets and novelists —like Tennyson and Dickens—fail in the drama, is because their habits of thought and methods of expression become fixed, and their genius cannot bring itself to yield to the unyielding domination of dramatic rule. And why should it? The world has gained, rather than lost, by their failures, for what they had to say was said in the appointed way.

The only career worth having as a dramatic writer is in original work. It is better to produce an honest drama—while in an avocation distinct from the stage—like Shiel, Talfourd, and others, than to be identified by trade-mark with the hand-me-downs of theatrical commerce.

No honest man writes hundreds of plays. It requires much less time to write a play in ordinary language than one of a high form of verse, where art goes to every syllable. Successful pieces have been conceived and written in a few weeks. Things have been thrown together in a few days. But these are not of the kind that stand publication. Publication would dismantle many a reputation nowadays, and lay bare the sources of his material. It is to be regretted that we no longer publish as the French continue to do.

Play construction requires time, and some writers reconstruct their plays many times.

Processes of construction may be traced in the life of Schiller, who left some pages of groundwork for certain of his dramas, finished and unfinished.

See also, as to the plotting of plays, the memoirs and lives of Coleman, Garrick, Macready, and others.

The younger writer should closely question all minor "laws," and accept with full intelligence and accord the general principles. He should not ground himself so in precedent that he cannot get away from it. In short, vigor in the place of imitation is the sure safeguard. Practice brings personal instinct. National instinct comes from universal observance on the stage of principle.

After all is said and done, the production of plays is a practical business. The young author should so regard it. Trials of a play, by way of mere curious experiment, a complaisance, are of little value in bringing it to use. Amateur acting and hasty staging are detrimental. A single performance is a gasp at life, and nothing more. Continuity of effort and life is the need.

There is no life more fragile than that of a dramatic infant. It requires nursing from the stage-manager and from the business charge. It is not property until it is listed with all formality in the dramatic market. It hardly has an existence until a manager is back of it with capital and the urgency of his convictions.

It all depends on a complex machinery. The commercial gentlemen who traverse the land are highly practical. They are dismayed by the bare manuscript. They handle successes by preference, and naturally enough. The producing manager in New York is limited to the policy of his house, its stage capacities, and so on. Thus it is absurd to send for perusal a tragedy to a manager whose company fits comedy only.

Plays often fail at first. Instance " The Colleen Bawn," "Private Secretary," "Pinafore," "School for Scandal," etc. A play is in production more than thrice refined; the author's inspiration, the actor's power, the manager's judgment, and the public's verdict. An author is the best judge of his own play. A sculptor knows if there is a flaw in his block of marble. An author that cannot decide on his own work is no author, and lacks the inner light. In other forms perhaps this does not hold, but in the drama it does, for it is in the material that all lies. One may not have this inner light, but as a professional he should have it.

The time required to write a play is entirely dependent on the man and the fullness and urgency of the idea in him, and like conditions. The old verse form would require longer to write than prose. Voltaire composed "Zaïre" in twenty-four days. Six months or a year give good assurance that the material of a play is well worked up. The actual writing may not have required a month. If you find that you cannot spend weeks and months on a play, ever with fresh enthusiasm or with persistent determination—if your resources of inquiry and mental combativeness desert you at the end of a week—it is possible that you have failed to grasp dramatic principle.

The young author usually writes a play not in touch with the times—which move so fast that a play of ten years ago would be of no use to-day.

Good plays are rare. Managers and the public, moreover, clamor for novelty. The reward is great, and the young author should reflect that technical excellence is indispensable.

It is sometimes said by managers and others that it is impossible to predict with any certainty the success of a play. This is in good part nonsense. It is true that by far the greater proportion of plays are experimental. Nor can the degree of success always be foretold. It takes very little to kill a play, but where every possible element is provided for a good drama, and where the result is the true effect of the play, and not the false conjunction of accidents and failures, one's preliminary judgment is as safe as the material.

This comment on a misleading saying does not, of course, intend to convey the statement that every man's judgment is true. It means simply that if the material is good, it can be passed upon in advance, just as gold can be. The truth is that the commercial manager does not care to risk his judgment.

The assay in the soul may be as firm as in

the public trial. A failure may be predicted with absolute sureness, and so with success. Failure at a first performance, owing to accident, and enduring favor on a revival, owing to truth, are common incidents in the history of the stage.

The laws of the stage are rarely felt in their full significance by one who first essays the drama. They meet with obstinate resistance; and what has been said should encourage a writer to closely revise his knowledge whenever and wherever a suggestion is made to him by his own failure, or by the wisdom, assumed or real, of his critics, managerial or journalistic.

CHAPTER XII.

THE LITERATURE OF DRAMATIC PRINCIPLE.

A BIBLIOGRAPHY of the drama, including history and biography, would be impracticable here by reason of its length, and, indeed, would not concern the technical elements of a play. Some works of the kind thus excluded may be referred to as belonging to the department of criticism, and helpful as models and indirect exponents of a science, essential to the well-being of the drama, to which a chapter has been devoted. Much reading is not required for the pursuit of any art. Knowledge of principle is alone sufficient to sustain any endeavor. A good actor does not derive his faculties from beholding the performances of others, and by virtue of his constant occupation is thrown upon his own resources; but principles he must know or must learn. Now, the technical elements of the drama have been fought for, and the books that have been foremost in the conflict are worth knowing something about. If one does not care to accept the statements herein, he is frankly and freely assisted in reaching the list of authorities. This book will then be found not to be a compilation, in the sense of being manufactured in a book-making spirit. While its very first words are the words of Aristotle, and while Hédelin and Diderot and Lessing and Schlegel and Freytag and others may share in its lines, there is a mutual and inevitable kinship in common principles. There is the breath of conflict in the book, conflict that concerns the good and evil in the drama of the present day. So that, after all, what is old and what is new in it is not to the point at all; and if the author has added anything new to the common fund, the recognition of that fact would be as nothing to him compared to the useful result that the book should accomplish in bringing home artistic truth to the right minds.

The preponderance of French works in the list demonstrates that books, or discussion in any form on principle and technique, are essential to the impression of the right thing not only on authors but on the people. The long French list is given partly with the view of making that point clear. It is true that, as has been said, where too much attention is given to form, the decadence of an art is indicated. Where by form conventionalism is meant, the saying is wholesome; but never if by the word form principle is intended. Never. More than this: the sooner we, as a people, get rid of the idea that genius disdains technique—that is, principle—the better for our development. All the really great dramatists have understood their art and have written about it—sometimes wrongly.

The beginning of the literature of dramatic principle is in Aristotle. His "Poetik" is brief and fragmentary, and treats only of tragedy, but he may be said to have created the firmament of drama in a critical way. The outlines are there. He lives. He is modern. He was misused in France, where from him were deduced the rules of the classic school. The treatise has been frequently translated into English, with notes. An available edition is that published in the Bohn Library.

The next period of written theory belongs to classic France. Its principles are summed up in a short treatise written by Abbé D'Aubignac, known as Hédelin, and which was translated into English many years ago, under a pretentious title, not the author's, as "The Whole Art of the Stage." In French, Chamfort's Dictionary goes more into detail under the various heads. Marmontel wrote many of the articles, which are reproduced in his collected works. In prefaces to their dramas, Corneille, Racine, and Voltaire ("Semiramis," etc.) wrote of principle with a good deal of fullness. Voltaire —whose hatred and misconception of Shakspere is known—has been brought into English in his "Discourse on Tragedy." Mercier's "Essai sur le Drame," not obtainable in this research, probably had the merit of first, among the French, discovering that the unity of interest was above the supposed necessities of time and place. With Diderot began—without much immediate result, for his plays were weak— some discernment that the classic school did not own mankind. This very practical, learned, common-sense, and able man claimed to have discovered and founded with his "Père de Famille" the *comédie larmoyante*, which is simply the domestic drama, and wrote strenuously in support of greater freedom in treatment. His "De la Poésie Dramatique" discusses his theories in a division into chapters that gives it the appearance of a convenient text-book. It was a book for the times, and, consequently, contains more about his own plays than serves just now. His analysis of a play, and his indication of mental processes and how to wrest the dramatic incidents and ideas from a theme, must be emphasized as very valuable to one looking into this subject.

Diderot, in discussing the plan, or the building-up, of a play, adopts the process of Aristotle, and illustrates by the following quotation from that great thinker:

"Whether you are working upon some well-known subject, or are attempting a new one, begin by mapping out the fable, and the episodes and incidents necessary for its development will occur to you. Is it a tragedy? Let us say, for example, that a princess is being led to the altar to be sacrificed,* but she vanishes suddenly and is transported to a country where it is the custom to sacrifice strangers to the goddess that is worshiped there. She is made a priestess. Some years later the brother of this princess comes to this country. He is seized by the inhabitants, and is on the point of being slain at the altar by the priestess, when he exclaims: 'It is not enough that my sister should have been sacrificed, for I, too, must be slain!' At these words he is recognized and saved. Now why had this princess been condemned to die on the altar? Why were strangers sacrificed in this barbarous land

* "Iphigenia," by Euripides.

where the brother encountered her? How was he captured? He came in obedience to an oracle. But wherefore this oracle? He was recognized by his sister, but could not this have been brought about in some other way? All of these incidents are lacking in the brief statement of the fable, and it is the poet's part to supply them. The story itself is common property."

Diderot then describes his own process with "Le Père de Famille":

"A father has two children, a son and a daughter. The daughter secretly loves a young man living in the same house. The son is infatuated with a girl of the neighborhood. He has sought to seduce her, but without success. He has disguised himself and settled down near her under an assumed name. He is there known as a mechanic of some kind. Occupied during the day, he can see the object of his passion only at night. But the father, watchful of what is going on in his house, learns that his son is absent every night. It is this conduct that introduces the derangement, the disquiet in the family affairs: he awaits his son.

"There the piece begins. What follows? He finds that the young girl is suitable for his son; and discovering at the same time that his daughter loves the young man for whom he has destined her, he arranges the two marriages, but against the consent of his brother-in-law, who has other plans. But why is it a secret love on the part of the young girl? How happens it that the young man she loves lives in the same house? What is he doing there? Who is he? Who is this unknown girl with whom the son is infatuated? How is it that she has fallen into her present state of poverty? Whence comes she? Born in the provinces, what has led her to Paris? What holds her there? Who is this brother-in-law? Upon what is based his authority in the household of this father? Why does he oppose these marriages that are agreeable to the father? But the action not being able to proceed in two places, how shall the young girl, the stranger, be introduced into the house of the family? How does the father discover the passion existing between his own daughter and the young man in the house? What reason has he for dissimulating his design? How does it happen that the girl, the young stranger, gains his approval? What are the obstacles that the brother-in-law brings to bear? How is the double marriage to be accomplished in spite of these obstacles?

"How many things remain undetermined even after the author has made his plot! But here you have the argument and the basis. Therefrom must be derived the division into acts, the number of characters, their individuality, and the nature of the scenes. I perceive that my plan is suitable, because the father, whose character I propose to depict, will encounter sorrow. He is to oppose a marriage suitable for his son; he is to see his daughter apparently withdrawn from a union that he desires for her, etc.

"The number of my characters is now to be decided. I am no longer uncertain about their individuality. The father shall have the characteristics of his station. He shall be good, vigilant, firm, and tender. Placed in the most difficult position of his life, his whole soul shall be engaged. It is necessary that his son shall be violent. The one he loves shall be innocent, true, and sensible. The brother-in-law, who is my mechanical lever, a narrow-minded man, full of prejudices, shall be stern, but weak, evil-minded, importunate, an intriguer, the bane of the house, the aversion of everybody.

"Who is this Germeuil? He is the son of a friend of the father, whom he has adopted after the death of the unfortunate man. Cécile, as well as Germeuil, while loving each other, are deferential in their relations, believing a union to be impossible under the circumstances. Thus Germeuil shall be self-composed but distant in manner. Cécile shall have pride, vivacity, reserve, and sensibility. The father shall fail to understand the situation at first; and the cross-purposes are established. . . . My purpose was to make the father the principal personage. The plot remained the same; but all the episodes would have been different if I had chosen for my chief character the son, the lover, or the uncle."

See also in Diderot's works his "Advice to a Young Man who proposed to write a Tragedy of Regulus."

In direct relation with Diderot stands Lessing, whose "Hamburgische Dramaturgie," epoch-making as to Germany, is the most substantial, the most honest, the most inspiring work ever done in the cause of the drama. It is not a formal treatise like Diderot's. Called to the Hamburg Theatre in 1767–69 to act as a kind of official critic, charged with educating the company as well as the public, for two years he published criticisms of the plays produced. He discussed all the material points in dramatic values just as he encountered them, irrespective of the attention excited by the play. The noble book outlives the temporal things in it. It grew up out of Lessing's fight for the true and the simple. It destroyed French supremacy and forced a new era for the German stage. It may be found translated in Bohn's edition. Written at a later period, Schlegel's "Lectures on Dramatic Art"—to be found in Bohn's edition—are at once brilliant and substantial. For the most part they concern the philosophy of the history of the drama in all nations, but he handles very freely some of the elements of dramatic principle. Sulzer's "Theorie der Kunst" is curiously careful and complete, German-like, for his day. It may be remarked in passing that nearly all works on æsthetics touch on the drama. In this way Hegel has some admirable chapters.

For the past generation, a book of large influence in Germany has been Freytag's "Technik des Dramas." This author, as dramatist and novelist, and after the German fashion thoroughly learned, was entirely competent to his task. His "Technik" is one of the very few that attempt to formulate. Its fault is too close an adherence to the Shaksperian form. His learning leads him into a deep study of the Greek, and thus he does not address himself

The Literature of Dramatic Principle. 253

sufficiently to the freedom from fixity that the present time demands.

Where the climax shall be and his complexity of "Stufungen" are not edifying. It is, however, a valuable standard work; and necessarily lays all subsequent writers under obligations, as have done before him all strong and independent thinkers on the subject.

Roescher, a voluminous German, is too metaphysical to be of value to all men. To many others it would be a loss of time to have recourse. Freytag, the brilliant author of one of the best novels of his century, "Soll und Haben," was followed by Spielhagen, another novelist, with "Beiträge zur Theorie und Technik des Romans." It is worth consulting in the obvious relations existing in creative art between the novel and the drama. It is in the form of critical essays.

English literature has little original material on dramatic principle. It is hardly worth the while to point out the fragmentary things of Dryden, Johnson, Addison, and many others, who have incidentally, and in prefaces and essays, touched on the subject. The literature does excel in picturesque history, biography, and critical comment. The critic's function has nowhere been better exercised. It is within the scope of this limited bibliography to refer to some of this material. Who has not read Lamb's delightful reminiscences of players, half-forgotten, some of them, but for him? William Hazlitt is particularly charming in a separate volume of republished criticisms written for newspapers, entitled "Views of the Stage."

Leigh Hunt and others will occur to any one. Dutton Cook's series of books, "Nights at the Play," "With the Players," "Hours with the Players," and "A Book of the Play," are interesting in their way.

William Archer is to be read. Joseph Hatton is admirable. It would be entering on a long list to refer to more than a few like Colly Cibber, Boaden, and Campbell, who in biographies have written delightfully, mainly of people, in a critical way. This field is too rich to more than hint at here. Criticism can find models of form and spirit there. A book of value, written in the manner of essays and without the purpose of a text-book, is Fitzgerald's "Principles of Comedy and Dramatic Effect." He very clearly defines and illustrates the lines of true comedy. The work has an honest purpose and is very entertaining. The same author's "On the Stage" grasps principle along with other comment. "Actors and the Art of Acting," by George

The Literature of Dramatic Principle. 255

Lewes, being largely critical reminiscence, contains useful observations on technique. See also the *variorum* editions of Shakspere. Critical matter of a like kind forms an interesting feature of French literature. In fact, for a long and unbroken period one may read criticisms, after the best skill of the day, on every piece of importance. Such criticisms are collected in Geoffrey's works. Grimm and La Harpe wrote thus. Jules Janin's criticisms are collected under the misleading title of "Histoire de la Literature Dramatique." See also Gautier and Jules Claretie, "La Vie Moderne au Théâtre," and "Causeries sur l'Art Dramatique," again a misleading title. Zola's collected criticisms, "Nos Auteurs," "Le Naturalisme au Théâtre," are in the main sound, as well as brilliant and effective.

He does not stand much, if any, below Janin. Should Francesque Sarcey publish his newspaper criticisms, there will be found a great fund of principle.

See also prefaces by Sardou and Dumas, and the preface by Victor Hugo to "Cromwell," in which he flays the unities.

This book of technique is concerned only with the text of operas, the libretto, the greatest writer of which was Scribe, whose methods are very plain in the slight text that requires to be expanded enormously with sound. Arteaga has written a history of opera. The triviality of the old librettos more than anything else led to the revulsion best expressed in Wagner. See his " Art Life and Theories," etc.; " Le Drame Musicale," by Edouard Schure; " The Story of the Opera," by W. D. Henderson, New York.

The history of the drama is part of the equipment of the critic and any man of letters, but it is not absolutely essential to the writer of plays after the modern methods and tendencies. If his material is strong within him, and his adherence to plain and simple principles firm enough, it little matters whether the author can speak by the book or not as to dates and persons. General histories of literature abound. Taine has special value in the matter of the drama. Ward's history comes down to Queen Anne. Klein in German is voluminous and comprehensive. Royer's "Histoire Universelle du Théâtre" gives full historical information. Prölls's "Geschichte des Neueren Dramas" is excellent; while Schlegel, up to the middle of the eighteenth century, is capital. Biographical histories abound, particularly in the English.

Concerning scenery or stage management, Becq de la Fouquière's book, " Art de la Mise

The Literature of Dramatic Principle. 257

en Scène" is good, but he stands too firmly, perhaps, on broad effects and the value of the painted over the practicable.

This author believes more in suggestion and the scene-painter than in realized detail. There is no doubt that some scenes can be realized only by the brush, such as the tessellated floor and the marble columns of an extensive palace interior. More than this, certain stone exteriors, as of a cathedral, or certain interiors, as of an old-fashioned dungeon, are peculiarly subject to the illusion afforded by the work of the skillful draughtsman and artist; but where the effects are not broad, as in a fashionable drawing-room of the present day, illusion is best served by an exact realization in a boxed interior of every detail of the life to be depicted. Even in action it is better in some cases to represent an army by having a few men constantly pass and repass a given point, where only the spear-points or gun-muzzles are seen over the top of a wall, than to attempt to fill the stage with incompetent supernumeraries. Thus the head of a column in the wings may suggest the head of an army. But stage possibilities are constantly widening. The theory of suggestion and that of realization do not necessarily conflict at all points. The union of the two methods was admirably demonstrated in the production of "The Great Metropolis," a play that has been done with great success in England and America. The shipwreck scene, devised by Mr. Teal, one of the authors, was indescribably effective, and yet the entire rescue of the persons from the ship beating to pieces in the breakers, with all the accompaniments of a great storm, was seen only in the intervals of the flashes of lightning.

Sanson also published "Observations sur l'Art de la Mise en Scène."

The infinite details of the principles and all that concerns the practical part of the stage and acting would seem to be covered by "Das Deutsche Theater Lexicon: Ein Encyclopedie alles Wissenswerthes der Schauspielkunst und Bühnentechnik; herausgegeben von Adolf Oppenheim und Ernst Gettke, unter mitwerkung Hervorragende Gelehete & Fach Maenner; 35 hefte, 1885–1888." Von Blum's "Theater Lexicon" seems to be of the same description. On examination of these books, however, one finds that they are largely biographical and historical. Pougin's Encylopedia is good. In English, Adam's "Dictionary of the Drama" is full of general historical information. See also magazine articles. Consult also "The Art of Authorship: Advice to Beginners, by Leading Authors," D. Appleton & Co.

The Literature of Dramatic Principle.

Two of the best satires ever written on conventionalism have recently appeared, in "Recettes de Cuisine Théâtrale," by Auguste Germaine, giving formulas for writing all kinds of plays; and "Stage Land," by Jerome K. Jerome, describing the characters commonly seen in dramas.

Referring the reader to Otto Lorenz's catalogue for French publications, to Heinsius for the German, and to the English trade catalogues, the writer will add a few titles, confessing at the same time small personal interest in the mere pursuit of books, and hoping that the man with a play in him ready to be written will stop short and forego the hunt; many of them have small value. Roumien, "L'Art Dramatique"; Cailhava, "De l'Art de la Comédie"; Horace's "Ars Poetica," in many translations. Boildieu's paraphrase and additions stand in far closer relation to the drama. Delsarte; Legouvé; "Essai d'une Bibliographie Générale du Théâtre"; "Dictionnaire de l'Art," etc., by Charles de Busney; "Essai sur l'Art Dramatique," par J. E. Aloux, 8vo, 1885; "Des Conditions de la bonne Comédie," par Karl Hillebrand, 8vo, 1863; Sanson's "L'Art Théâtrale," acting; Talma, "Reflections sur le Kain et l'Art Théâtrale"; Diderot's "Essay on the Actor's Art"; Riccaboni; Beaumarchais; Hutton's "Plays and Players";

Brown's, Dunlop's, Ireland's " Histories of the American Stage"; "Poole's Index" (and the like current ones) to magazine articles, which are usually of no value; but Boucicault in the *North American Review* (Jan. 1878) and Julian Magnus in *Lippincott* are excellent in the matter of the construction of plays. La Rousse's " Dictionnaire" of the French language is uncommonly full and satisfactory in its definitions and in its account of works bearing on the drama.

In the matter of reading, men differ in their habits and in their receptivity, but he alone can read with profit and discrimination who is first grounded in principle.

INDEX.

Acceptability, a decisive element in the drama, 30.
Accident, forbidden by cause and effect, 110.
Action, a complete, defined, Chapter I.; see also Chapter IV.
Actor, the, incidental references to, 31, 38, 46, 68, 115, 118, 121, 123, 126, 127, 131, 134, 135, 136, 146, 149, 150, 154, 155, 156, 162, 164, 166, 173, 211, 217, 219, 235, 236, 243.
Acts, the division into, Chapter IV., 65; three natural parts, beginning, middle, and end, 65; no other arbitrary rule, 65; five acts not imperative, 65; not known to early drama, 65; this division explained, 65; usually some happening in the interval, 66; always a new relation after each, 66; a place to bestow events impracticable in the acting, and the like, 66; thus hastening on, 66; periods of rest, 67; but a long play possible without them, 68; a saying of the elder Dumas, 68; a misapprehension, 68; lapse of time provided for, 69; present distinct pictures and help the memory, 70; sometimes compelled by scenic requirements, 70; for plays constructed, not written, 70; each to accomplish something definite, 70; and may be entitled accordingly, 72; no uniform length or time for, 70; but according to its function, 71; an articulated part of a play, 70; Corneille's uniformity in, 71; action, beginning of, middle of, rise and decline of, introduction, exposition, development, climax, denouement, catastrophe, and end, touched on, 71; plot, 72; story, 73; Brougham's saying, "A play writes itself," 73; derived from laws of human nature, 73; a plot is the solution of a prob-

lem, 73; not to be a puzzle, 74; the simple and complex, 74; compared with composition in painting, 74; action placed above emotion and character, 74; the requirements of a plot, 75; the underplot, 75; the scenes and the plot inherent in the subject, 74; unfolding of, 74; perspicuity in, 75; should be susceptible of brief statement, 75; illusion destroyed by weakness of treatment, 75; introduction, the, 76; laying the foundation, 76; natural order of the action and statement of facts, 76; the same as in telling an anecdote, 76; facts to be stated or withheld, 77; economic value of scenery as to such statement, 78; proceeding in the exposition and introduction from the general to the particular, 78; as seen in "The Two Orphans," 78; D'Ennery's development of character, 78; relations between characters, 79; motives, promises, and possibilities lie here, 79; curiosity and interest to be aroused, 80; the clash, or real beginning of action, 80; functions of the first act, or, more properly, of the beginning, 80; preparation for future scenes, as in "The Two Orphans," 80; character may be identical with action, 80; sympathies, or interest, to be directed and husbanded, 80; action to be unfolded out of present relations, 81; the spoken prologue, 81; recital of incidents, should be a part of the action, 81; as in "Othello," 81; "Hamlet," 82; and "Daniel Rochat," 82; introduction should gain confidence and pleasure of audience, 83; clearness, 83, 85; tardy explanations fatal, 84; preparation—a better term than "motive"—the solvent, as in "A Scrap of Paper," 83; spectator is part author, 84; preparation explains in a flash, 84; illusion is preoccupation of the mind, 85; interest possible even when we know every incident in advance, 85; suspense, 85; weighing effects, 85; what to state and what to act, 86; "A Scrap of Paper," 86; "The Silver King," 87; "A Celebrated Case," etc., 87; authors must note effects like a painter, 86; touch of, 86; over-elaboration, 87; when statement more effective than "action," 87; false rule as to quiet beginning, 87; "Othello,"

88; "Romeo and Juliet," 88; preparation, 89; relative value of facts, 89; inordinate introduction and exposition, 89; material faulty, 89; essential facts to be in the introduction, 89; these dictated by the material, 89; first act to be a completed standpoint, 89; introductory matter extending through three acts of "The Two Orphans," 89; style and tone seen in introduction, 89; the clash, and beginning of action, 90; "Richard III." and "Julius Cæsar," 90; no absolute rule as to introduction of characters, 90; Shakspere sometimes includes all in first act, 90; but characters may exist before or without being seen, 91; "Rob Roy," "Mary Stuart," 91; prologue, often essential, 91; "Monte Cristo," "Jane Eyre," 91; danger of its differing in tone from the play, 91; material from real life best, 92; what to state, 92; introduction may of necessity be tedious, 92; recital, narrative to be made by right people, as in "A Scrap of Paper," 92; action to be foreshadowed, 92; right people to say the right things, 92; conventional beginnings, 93; curiosity and interest the function of the first act, 94; introduction, conciliatory, agreeable, 92; semiclassic rules at fault in opening, 92; principles rather than laws, 93; conventionalism, certain bits of, well enough, 93; the feather duster, 93; illusion, 93; recital, two men seated in chairs, 93; expectation, suspense, satisfaction, are the three parts of a play, 93; functions of Act I., interest and curiosity, 94. Act II., development, 94; a second definite step forward, 94; characters, 95; "Daniel Rochat," 95; "The Danicheffs," 95; "The Courier of Lyons," cited, 95; clash illustrated, 95; climax, 96; interest cumulative, 96; proportions, no fixed, but important, 96; situation, illustrated from "Fate," 97; curiosity, 98; interest to exist everywhere, 98; must be sustained by devices, 98; character, 99; plot, 99; action, 99; situation defined, 99; suspense emphasized by situation, 99; "Jim the Penman" and "Diplomacy," 99; complications, 100. Act III., the crisis or climax, 100; "The Courier of Lyons," 101; "Article 47," 101; "The Danicheffs," 101; "Daniel Rochat," 102;

"Camille," 102; wrought-up action is no true climax, 102; stolen climaxes, 102; not necessarily explosive or "powerful," 103; anti-climax, 103; "Daniel Rochat" and Dumas, etc., 103. Act IV., denouement, 105; solution of the plot, 105; fulfilling the promises, 106; not to be sudden, 106; vigor in denouement even in "Daniel Rochat," 106; the solvent nature of, illustrated from Macbeth, 107; action still important, 107; difficulty of sustaining interest, 108; "A Parisian Romance," 108; the end foreshadowed, 108; "The Courier of Lyons," 108; retardation, 108; "The Two Orphans," 109. Act V., the conclusion, must be a logical result, and a definite ending, 109; in tragedy the shadow of the ending deepens, 110; "Julius Cæsar," "Richard III.," and "Romeo and Juliet," 110; accident a poor device, 111; "Rent Day," 111; play really ends when interest ends, 111; further illustration, 111.

Adams's "Dictionary of the Drama" referred to, 258.

Adaptation and dramatization, Chapter VIII., 178; a necessity for the manager, 178; Wallack's error, 179; A. M. Palmer's success, 179; changes made in "The Banker's Daughter" and "The Two Orphans," 179; adapter often a marplot, 180; mere translation not adaptation, 180; when this is obvious, 181; "Duprez and Son," 180; Charles Reade's scorn of the adapter, 181; Daly's "Lottery of Love," 181; mistake in adaptation of D'Ennery's "Martyr," 182; true adaptation requires skill, 182; Robertson's "Caste" and "School," 182; Molière's "Tartuffe," as the "Non-juror," "The Serious Family," and "The Colonel," 182; English provincialism in, 182; "The Banker's Daughter," adapted by Alberry, 182; the Palgrave Simpsons and Sydney Grundys, 183; Joseph Jefferson and his adaptation of "The Rivals," 183-188; dramatization, may involve great skill, but is generally patchwork, 188; best to break into pot metal, 188; internal evidences of a novel, 188; the plunderer, 188; difficulty as to popular novels, 188; must be complete within itself, 189; "Camille," 189; custom of French authors, 189;

examples of good work in adaptation, 189; the critic never deceived in stolen plays, 190.
"Adonis," cited in illustration, 198.
"Adrienne," cited in illustration, 194.
Æsthetics; see "The Three Elements of a Drama," Chapter II., 20, 27.
"Alabama," referred to, 14.
Alberry, James, referred to, 182.
Allusion, forbidden in some forms, permitted in others, 126, 196.
American Stage, histories of the, by Dunlap, Ireland, and Brown, 260.
Anecdote in the nature of the dramatic, 11.
Anticipation; see the Introduction, 76.
Anti-climax, a lesser interest following a greater, as in rhetoric, 103.
"Antony and Cleopatra," cited, 122.
"Apology for poetry," by Sir Philip Sidney, cited, 31.
Archer, William, referred to, 254.
Aristotle, 1, 3, 39, 40, 55, 59, 60, 65, 158, 159, 192, 244, 245, 246.
"Art of Authorship," title cited, 258.
Art, the elimination of the non-essential; to produce desired effects; dramatic, uses all other arts: 18, 38, 52, 53, 56, 150, 243.
Arteaga, history of opera, referred to, 256.
"Article 47," cited, 38, 101, 125, 132.
Asides, a natural device, particularly in comedy, 127.
"As You Like It," cited, 78, 152, 172, 181.
"Athalie," cited, 194.
Audience, part author of a play, etc., 3, 18, 28, 58, 59, 77, 83, 84, 85, 87, 117, 137, 152, 154, 173.
Author, advice to, Chapter XI., 224; see also 12, 14, 28, 70, 72, 74, 77, 81, 86, 114, 115, 116, 118, 130, 131, 132, 134, 166, 170, 191; fallacy that the author should be an actor, 236.

Ballet, 39, 200.
Banim, " Damon and Pythias," 104, 138.
" Banker's Daughter, The," cited, 14, 117, 179, 182.
Barrett, Wilson, play cited, 139.
Beaumont and Fletcher, play cited, 189.
Becq de la Fouquière, book on stage management, 256.
Beginning of play and of action, 3, 88, 232.
Bellinghausen, M. von, " Ingomar," 172.
Bélot, plays by, cited, 23, 38, 101, 125, 132.
Benedix, his book against Shakspere, 218.
Bible, the, like the drama, depicts vice, 29.
Boaden, referred to, 254.
Boildieu, referred to, 259.
Books on the drama, Chapter XII., 243.
Booth, Edwin, referred to, 173.
Boucicault, 45, 167, 189, 260.
Bourgeoise, play by, cited, 208.
" Bridal, The," referred to, 189.
Brougham, a saying by, 73, 184.
Buchanan, Robert, play cited, 172.
Buckstone, referred to, 189.
Bulwer, plays by, cited, 37, 96, 104, 115, 127, 172, 205.
Bunn, Alfred, a bit of stage management, 120.
Burlesque, 196.
Business; see Chapter V., 112, 131.

" Cabale und Liebe," cited, 11.
Cailhava, " De l'Art de la Comédie," referred to, 259.
" Camille," cited, 23, 61, 75, 102, 155, 163, 189.
Campbell, Bartley, referred to, 14, 97.
Campbell, Thomas, referred to, 254.
" Caste," cited, 82, 101, 155, 168, 174, 182.
Catastrophe, Chapter IV., 109.
Cause and effect, pervades the drama, 6.
" Celebrated Case, A," 61, 85, 87, 115, 153, 189.
Chamfort, his dictionary referred to, 245.

Character, Chapter VI., 149; a prevailing trait necessary, 149; old descriptiveness in names, 149; Massinger's "New Way to Pay Old Debts," 149; lines of business, 150; what a man's character is, 150; must be consistent, etc., 150; dramatic unity of, 151; all dramatic principles apply to, 151; morality in dramatic character, 151; may be created in few strokes, 151; Adam in "As You Like It," cited, 151; must be revealed very soon, 152; must not be merely described, but what others say is helpful, 152; Shakspere's methods, 152; how impressed, 152; probability, 152; motive, 153; as contributed to by scenery, 153; dress, 153; Sir Pertinent McSycophant, 154; plays of character, 154; often left to actor, 154; few characters needed for use in action, 154; a character created for a special scene, 155; incidental figures, 155; "The Two Orphans," cited, 156; supers, 156; economy in, 157; not two for one, 157; double characters, as in "Hamlet," "Macbeth," "Romeo and Juliet," 157; Aristotle's mixed good and evil in, 158; must entertain, 158; "Othello," cited, 158; conventionalism of reuniting at the end, 159; "Fernande," cited, 159; Aristotle's rules of character, 159; vice as depicted in, 159; must do what is expected of them, 160; character must soon appear, 160; metaphysics not needed in devising characters, 161; see also Chapters IV. and V.; entrance and exit, 78; certain tricks of, 161; should never be made on a pretext not verified, 162; preparation of character for, 162; contrast an element not absolutely and always necessary, 163; stage humor as it differs from literary, 163; conventional types sometimes unavoidable, 164; the comedy of character, 164; falsities in one-part comedies, 164; melodramatic, 164, 250.

Children as figures in the drama, 164.
Cibber, Colly, commended for reading, 254.
"Cid, The," referred to, 32.
Cities, the drama a requirement of life in, 16.
Claretie, Jules, his criticisms referred to, 255.
Clash, the, the kindling point of every drama, 80, 90, 94, 95.

Clearness, a matter-of-course requirement, 83, 84, 166.
Climax, 8, 71, 72, 95, 101, 102, 103, 104, 105.
Collins, Wilkie, his process in constructing a plot, 230; "The New Magdalen," 23.
Comedy, and comedy interest, 16, 17, 29, 30, 120, 164, 194.
Common sense, the basis of play-writing, 230.
Comparison, a rhetorical device not permitted by Corneille, 126.
Confidence, to be gained in the beginning, 83.
Conflict, the soul of the drama, 5.
Congruity, an element of unity, 57.
Consistency; see Unity and Character.
Contrast, 29, 123, 163, 167.
Conventionalism, 43, 45, 53, 54, 93, 159, 164, 202.
Cook, Dutton, his books referred to, 259.
Corneille, and the rules of the classic school, 32, 41, 60, 61, 71, 126, 246.
"Corsican Brothers, The," cited, 104.
Coup-de-Théâtre, 84.
"Courier of Lyons, The," Moreau, Siraudin, and Delacour, cited, 87, 95, 101, 108, 168, 174, 175.
Courtney, John, "Damon and Pythias," 104.
Coyne, Sterling, referred to, 190.
"Critic, The," cited, 97.
Criticism, Chapter X., 212; should be mainly by way of encouragement, 212; should combat real evils only, 212; should reproduce public impressions, 213; should be sincere, 213; Charles Lamb's criticism of Mrs. Jordan's Viola, 213; should not disdain sentiment, 214; essential to public morals and taste; to managers as well, 215; Winter, Hazlitt, Lamb, Clement Scott, Le Maitre, and Sarcey, 215; difficulties of, 216; should sustain adverse criticism by proof, 217; should treat each play after its kind, 217; should heed honest criticism, 217; hypercriticism, 218; Benedix's book against Shakspere, 218; unimportant plays often require criticism, 218; value of rural criticism, 219; not necessary to criticise everything, 223; mere knowledge of local facts

Index. 269

and dates about plays not criticism, 59, 173, 190, 191, 222; see also Chapter XII.
" Crockett, Davy," referred to, 14.
" Curiosities of the American Stage," by Hutton, 197.
Curiosity, an element, 84, 85, 94, 98, 111, etc.
" Cymbeline," cited, 27.

Daly, Augustin, plays by, cited, 83, 104, 181.
" Damon and Pythias," cited, 104, 138.
" Danicheffs, The," 95, 101, 174.
" Daniel Rochat," 75, 82, 95, 102, 106, 125, 155.
" Danites, The," referred to, 14.
D'Aubignac, Abbé (Hédelin), an authority on dramatic law of the period of Corneille, 51, 245.
" Daughter of Roland," cited, 116.
Delay, an element of the action, 100, 122.
" Demetrius," referred to, 57.
" Denise," an impracticable theme, 21.
D'Ennery, a master of construction, play by him, cited, 22, 61, 76, 78, 84, 89, 109, 115, 156, 179, 180, 182, 189, 193.
Denouement, 105, and Chapter IV.
Description; see Recital.
Development, Chapter IV., 65, 72, 94.
Dialogue, its requirements and uses, 118, 121, 122, 123, 124, 126, 160.
Dickens, Charles, why he was not successful in the drama, 188, 237.
Diderot, 244; his " De la Poésie Dramatique," 246; his process in building up his play " Le Père de Famille," 251, 259.
" Diplomacy," referred to, 99.
Dixey, H. E., in a representative "farce comedy," 198.
Drama, definition of, Chapter I., 1; what is dramatic, 2; a reflex of life, 2; modern themes best, 2, 4; the idea must be capable of form, 2; action must be complete, 2; logical, 2; perfection the aim, 2; must be organic, 2; and possess unity, 2; invite sympathetic attention and maintain interest

to the end, 2; its heart, emotion, 3, 5; has limitations, 3; a beginning, as in "Romeo and Juliet," 3; to be acted in given time, 6; cause and effect, 6; proportionate parts, 6; to progress by action, 6, 12; probability, 7; the merely theatric, 8; intensity not a general law, 9; the anecdote is a drama, 11; farce comedies, 12; the germ, 11; not complete till acted, 8; like a case at law, 9; suspense, 9; progression, 9; true drama bounded on all sides by fact, 13; the historical, 13; illusion, 13; dramatizations, 13; the theme, 7, 13; general and particular, 7; an object required, 7; native subjects, 12; the rogue writes foreign plays, 13; why the French author is strong, 13; but drama universal, 14; Shakspere, 14; other requirements to be noted hereinafter, 16.

Drama, the three elements of a, Chapter II., 20; they determine the availability of the theme, 20; the ethical, the æsthetic, the technical, 20. I. The ethical, 20; the object of a drama must accord with popular moral views, 20; object unavoidable, 21; bad object may destroy dramatic quality, 21; Dumas's "Denise," 21; D'Ennery's "Martyr," 22; vice as depicted on the stage, 22; distinctions, 23; "Forget-me-Not," "Camille," "Frou Frou," "New Magdalen," 23; "Harvest," 25, 77; "Fazio," "Measure for Measure," 27; "Cymbeline," 27; "La Tosca," 27; "Faust," 27; "Mousetrap," 26; if premises not accepted must be proved, 23; moral prejudice of the day may be wrong, 27; technique cannot establish moral law, 27; principles change, 27; Rome's Coliseum, 27; each age sets up its standards, 28; illusion depends on moral agreement of audience with the play, 28; to excite discussion fundamentally wrong, 28. II. The æsthetic, 29; the term includes the obvious law that a play must entertain, 30; what Goethe says, 30; taste offended by bad morals and bad technique, 30; pleasure does not depend on laughter only, 30; bad taste in play, cited, 32; bad theory that the public must take care of itself, 31; Dryden's failure in theory as to comedy, 31; murderer in love with his victim's daughter, cited, 31; Gwynne, 33; plays on such themes are not plays, 35; trying to make a silk purse out of a sow's ear, 35; villainy rightly used need not offend taste, 35; even the villain must entertain, 35; bad taste illustrated by examples from various plays, 36–38; good acting can never redeem bad taste, 38; terror, pity, etc., in tragedy referred back to other treatises, 39; the physically æsthetic part may be the charm, as in verse or music, 39; books of philosophy not needed to study taste, 38; must be inherent, 38; the drama not the stuff of a moment's fancy, 39. III. Technical, the, 39; the art of giving form, 39; not fixed, like mathematics, 40; its general laws as steadfast as nature, 40; the structure of theatres influences, 40; Greek drama, cited, 40; also whims of managers various, and changing elements of, 41; fixed forms, 41; emancipation of, 42; freedom permissible, 42; accuracy essential, 43; the theme first, 43; skill next, 43; illustrated by painting, 43; first step is to ascertain values, 43; illusion, and not appreciation by public of the art, the dramatist's concern, 44; each form has its laws, 45; instinct better than rule, 45; Goldsmith, etc., 45; conventionalism, 45; individuality in, 46; Sheridan's lack of skill in "School for Scandal," 46; but genius works by rule, 50; art as genuine as nature, 52; technique alone cannot write plays, but great French writers become technical, 52; the earnest cultivation of art in France, 52; Legouvé's belief in the mathematics of the drama, 53; constant improvement in, 54; the folly of conventionalism, 55.

Drama, forms of, Chapter IX., 191; some extinct, 191; new constantly arising, 191; confusion as to critics and authors, 191; tragedy defined, 192; the inevitable in, 192; "Romeo and Juliet," "Macbeth," "Hamlet," "Othello," "Richard III.," 192; Aristotle's definition, 192; mirth unknown in pure tragedy, 193; contrast in, 193; "The Two Orphans," thorough melodrama cited on this point, 193; love-interest not necessary to tragedy, "Macbeth," "Lear," "Julius Cæsar," "Athalie," 193; but Schiller's "Wallenstein," 194;

"Venice Preserved," "Adrienne," 194; comedy defined, 194; painful scenes to be avoided, 195; "School for Scandal," "She Stoops to Conquer," 195; pure comedy concerns character and must be natural, 195; various forms of, 196; artificial comedy, 196; burlesque, 196; its characteristics, 196; *farce*, almost extinct, 196; John Maddison Morton, 196; negro minstrels, 197; farce comedy, ill named, American in origin, 197; Hoyt, 197; illustrated by Dixey's "Adonis," 198; "Bunch of Keys," 198; Dr. Mulo Medicus, 198; German comedy, Moser, 199; spectacular pieces, 199; opera, 200; Scribe as librettist, 200; vaudeville, 200; pantomime, 200; ballet, 200; Offenbach, 201; opera bouffe and opera comique, 202; Gilbert and Sullivan, 202; "Pinafore," "Mikado," "Ruddygore," 202; historical plays, 204; difficulties of, 204; romantic melodrama, 205; English melodrama, 206; probabilities in "Lagardere," 207; crime in melodrama, 207; suspense in, 208; morals and taste in, 209; romanticism not mere complication, 210; "Paul and Virginia," "Picciola," cited, 210; the preponderance of some one element creates forms, 210; forms for the eye, ear, imagination, etc., 211; numberless, 211; art would fare better with a repertory theatre, 211.

Drama, the use of, 16; essential to civilization, particularly in large cities, 16; preaches and teaches in a dramatic way, 17; entertainment not its only function, 17; falsity of the saying "People do not want to think," 18; the boy understands "Richard III." without "thinking," 18; drama involves all arts, 18; the absolute practical value of, 19.

Drama, books on the, Chapter XII., 243; see Dramatic Principle.

"Drama, French's Standard," commended for reference, 21, 189.

Drama, how built up, Chapter XI., 224; see Play.

Dramatic principle, the literature of, Chapter XII., 244; much reading not required for any art, 244; the French excel in the discussion of the drama, 245; Aristotle's "Poetik," 245;

Hédelin, Chamfort, and Marmontel, who with Corneille, Racine, and Voltaire wrote from the classic standpoint, 246; Mercier's essay, 246; Diderot's "De La Poésie Dramatique," 246; he quotes Aristotle's analysis, 247; describes his own process in play-writing, 248; Lessing's great polemic "Dramaturgie," 251; Schlegel's "Lectures," 252; Freytag's "Technik," 252; other German writers, 252; critical essayists and biographers in England, Archer, Hatton, Cibber, Boaden, and Campbell, 254; Fitzgerald's "Comedy and Dramatic Effect," 254; George Lewes on "Actors and the Art of Acting," 254; the French critics, Grimm, La Harpe, Jules Janin and Claretie, 255; Zola's excellent volumes, 255; Sardou and Dumas in prefaces, 255; Victor Hugo's preface to "Cromwell," 255; histories and discussions of the opera, 256; histories of the stage, Taine, Ward, Klein, Royer, Prölls, and Schlegel, 256; Becq de la Fouquière's book, "Art de la Mise en Scène," 256; its opposition to realism, 257; Sanson's book, 258; dictionary, 258; two books of satire, by Germaine and Jerome, 259; a short list of other works, 259; an article of value by Boucicault, 260; see also "Précis de Dramatique," by Viollet-Le-Duc; and "Why I don't write Plays," *Pall Mall Budget*, beginning with September, 1892.

Dramatization; see Adaptation and, Chapter VIII., 178, 188.

"Dramaturgie, Hamburgische," Lessing's great work, 60, 251.

Dumas, plays by, cited, and other references to, 21, 23, 68; an anecdote of the elder, 75, 95, 102, 103, 124, 155, 163, 169, 174; gives proportion as the main factor in the drama, 189, 236.

"Duprez and Son," cited, 180.

"Elaine," cited, 144.
Emotion, when it is dramatic, 10.
Emphasis, 80, 87.
End, Chapter IV., 65; 5, 57, 109.
Enthusiasm, a quality of receptivity to be fostered, 221.
Entrance, Chapter VI., 149; 161.

Episode, 58, 110, 129, 130.
Ethical, the, Chapter II., 20.
" Eustace Baudin," 61, 82, 85, 155, 160, 172.
Exit, Chapter VI., 149; 135, 161.
Expectation, must exist always, 93, 98, 175.
Explanation, 84, 128.
Exposition, Chapter IV., 65; 76.

Facts, relative value of, 77, 81, 84, 85, 86, 89; drama bounded by fact, 13.
Farce, its nature, 196.
Farce comedy, an American product, 120, 197.
" Fate," cited, 97.
" Faust," cited, 120; Irving's stage management in "Faust" equivalent to authorship, 147.
" Fazio," Milman, cited, 27.
" Fedora," cited, 32.
Feuillet, plays by, cited, 35, 106, 167.
Féval, play by, cited, 208.
Fitzgerald, 176; his " Principles of Comedy and Dramatic Effect," etc., 254.
Focus, determines the unity, so that the focus of the play not the focus of the novel, 81, 126.
" Forget-Me-Not," cited, 23.
Freedom, with just technique; see preface and 42, 43, 46.
French, the, as a nation skilled in technique, and why, 15, 52, 244.
Freytag, his " Technik des Dramas " commended, 244, 252, 253.
" Frou Frou," cited, 23, 27.

Gautier, referred to as a critic, 255.
Geoffroy, French critic, 255.
Germ of a play, 7, 10, 20, 227.
Germaine, Auguste, " Recettes de Cuisine Théâtrale," a satire on the effete, 259.

Index. 275

Gilbert and Sullivan, creators of a new form, 13, 202, 236.
Gillette, "Held by the Enemy," 14.
"Gisippus," cited, 98.
Goethe, referred to, and plays cited, 27, 30, 32, 236; consult also Eckermann's "Gespräche" and "Wilhem Meister."
Goldsmith, an artist by instinct, 45; plays cited, 190, 195.
Greek drama, 40.
Griffin, Gerald, "Gisippus," 98.
Groups, use of, 128.
Grundy, Sydney, 183.

Halévy, "Frou Frou," 23, 27, and associated with Offenbach, 201.
Hamilton, Henry, author of "Harvest," 25.
"Hamlet," cited, 35, 82, 127, 140.
"Harvest," cited, 25, 35, 37, 157, 192.
Harvey, Frank, his characteristic English melodramas, 206.
Hatton, Joseph, referred to, 254.
"Hazel Kirke," its frequent revision after production, 229.
Hazlitt, William, his dramatic criticisms, 214, 254.
"Heart's-ease," cited, 23.
Hédelin; see D'Aubignac, 244.
Hegel, and other writers on the æsthetic, on the drama, 252.
"Held by the Enemy," referred to, 14.
Henderson, W. J., "The Story of the Opera," 256.
"Henrietta, The," cited, 195.
Historical, the, limitations of its use, 13, 129, 188, 204.
"Honeymoon, The," cited, 51, 118, 165, 174, 206.
Horace, his "Ars Poetica" referred to, 259.
Howard, Bronson, referred to, and plays cited, 14, 39, 117, 141, 179, 182, 195, 236.
Hoyt, Charles, the chief of American farce-makers, 197.
Hugo, Victor, plays by, cited, and his fight against the classic, 32, 41, 60, 206, 255.
Humor, its dramatic uses, 157, 163, 164.
"Hunchback, The," cited, 84.

Hunt, Leigh, his essays referred to, 254.
Hutton, Lawrence, "Curiosities of the American Stage," 197.
Hutton's "Plays and Players," 259.

Illusion, the aim of the drama, 66, 68, 142, 169.
Imagination, the, of the spectator to be invoked, 66, 69.
Impressions, the test of a play, 20, 88.
Incidents, should not be too few or too many, 87.
Individuality, 46.
"Infatuation," cited, 172.
"Ingomar," cited, 172.
Instinct, dramatic, 45.
Intelligibility, 166.
Intensity, the tendency, but not the sole requirement of the drama, 9.
Interest, to exist throughout, 71, 85, 98, 99, 111.
Introduction, Chapter IV., 65, 76–94.
Irving, Henry, some of his theory and practice, 120, 146, 147, 173, 190.

"Jane Eyre," cited, 91.
Janin, Jules, his collected criticisms, 255.
Jefferson, Joseph, his remarkable adaptation of "The Rivals," 183.
Jerome, his "Stage Land," a satire on the effete, 259.
Jerrold, Douglas, play by, cited, 111.
"Jim the Penman," cited, 99, 100, 176.
Jones, Henry Arthur, plays by, cited, 87, 139, 236.
Jonson, Ben, inclined to observe the unities, 60.
"Julius Cæsar," cited, 90, 110, 130, 194.

Klein's "History of the Drama," 256.
Knowles, Sheridan, plays by, cited, 84, 87, 189, 205.
Kotzebue, his "Stranger," cited, 23.
"Kreutzer Sonata, The," why it offends, 30.

"Lady of Lyons, The," cited, 37, 96, 104, 172, 205.
"Lagardere," or "The Duke's Motto," cited for its romanticism, 207.
La Harpe, referred to, 215.
Lamb, Charles, a charming bit of criticism by, 213, 254.
Language, 166.
"La Tosca," the question involved in, 27.
"Lear," love-interest lacking in it, and not essential, 193.
"Led Astray," referred to, 167.
Legouvé, his statement as to the mathematics of the drama, 53; "Adrienne," 194.
Le Maitre, a master in criticism, 215.
Length of a play, 6.
Length of a scene or act, 71, 113, 118.
Lessing, plays by, cited, and recognition made of service to the drama, 36, 42, 60, 158, 236, 244, 251.
Lewes, George, "Actors and the Art of Acting," 254.
Limitation, 1, 3, 6, 31, 32, 42.
Literature of Dramatic Principle, Chapter XII., 243.
"Lord Harry, The," its excessive scenery, 139.
"Lottery of Love, The," cited, 181.
"Love Chase, The," cited, 171, 205.
Love-interest, Corneille thought it subordinate, 54; the demand that it exist in every play is absurd, 193.

"Macbeth," cited, 107, 157, 164, 192, 193.
MacKaye, Steele, author of "Hazel Kirke," 229.
Macready, adaptation by, 189.
Magnus, Julian, article by, commended, 260.
"Maid's Tragedy," adapted from Beaumont and Fletcher, 189.
Management, 178, 236.
Mansfield, Richard, 108.
"Marble Heart," cited, 82.
Marmontel, representing the technique of the classic period, 246.
"Martyr," cited, 22, 115, 182.
Masses, the use of, 129.

Massinger, 149, 151.
Material, its value and controlling influence, 7, 12, 43, 63.
McEntee, Jervis, artist of sentiment, 44.
" Measure for Measure," cited, 27, 133.
Melodrama, defined, 205, 206.
Mercier, " Essai sur le Drame," 246.
Merivale, " Forget-Me-Not," 23.
" Metropolis, The Great," Jessup and Teal, cited for its stage management, 258.
" Mikàdo, The," 13, 202.
Miller, Joaquin, author of " The Danites," 14.
" Miss Multon," cited, 23.
Molière, cited, 182, 236.
Monologue, 127.
Monotony, a dramatic crime, 169.
" Monte Cristo," why the prologue is required, 91.
Morality, in character; see Chapter II., *passim*.
Morton, J. Maddison, the master of farce, 196.
Moser, Gustave, his methods referred to, 199.
Motives, 84, 171, 176; see also Proportion and Character.
" Mousetrap, The," an example of falsity, 26, 35.
" My Partner," referred to, 14.

" Nathan the Wise," cited, 36.
Naturalism, 146.
Negro minstrelsy, 197.
" New Way to Pay Old Debts, A," cited, 149.
Novels, 13, 188.

Object, inevitable in the drama, 7, 20, 27.
" Œdipus," a theme peculiar to its period, 32.
Offenbach, his creation of a new form, 201.
" Old Homestead, The," cited, 119, 130.
" Old Love and the New, The," cited, 117.
" Olivia," as an adaptation, 190.
Opera, 200; opera-bouffe, 202.

Organic, the; see specially Chapters I. and III.
Originality, a misused term, 12.
"Othello," cited, 36, 81, 88, 158, 192.
Otway, author of "Venice Preserved" and "The Orphan," 194.
Over-elaboration, 139, 145.

Padding, a literary vice, insufferable in the drama, 131.
Painting, points of identity in technique, 89, 165.
Palmer, A. M., the skillful and successful adaptations made under his direction, 117, 178, 182; see also plays produced by: "The Two Orphans," "A Celebrated Case," "The Banker's Daughter," "The Danicheffs," "Led Astray," "Daniel Rochat," "A Parisian Romance," etc.
Pantomime, as a form, 200; as incidental to the action and expression, 120, 126, 129.
"Parisian Romance, A," cited, 108.
"Pattes de Mouche"; see "A Scrap of Paper," 11, 83.
Perspicuity, 165.
"Pinafore," referred to, 202.
Planché, referred to, 196.
Play, the building up of a, Chapter XI., 224; principle, and not a model, should be the guide, 224; mere dry rule of no value, 224; common sense at the bottom of all playwriting, 225; the art may be taught, 225; writing plays a proper exercise for any literary student, 226; the significance of a successful play, 226; impossible to hide weakness in a play, 226; analysis of plays commended, 226; the author, 227; mental processes, 227; the germ, 227; Schiller's "Cabale und Liebe," 227; gestation required, 228; mastery of the theme of first importance, 228; selection and rejection of material, 228; weighing effects, 228; "Hazel Kirke," cited, 229; constructed, not written, 229; Wilkie Collins's analysis of his mental process with his novel "The Woman in White," 230; Ibsen's experience, 234; how characters arise and are developed, 235; general plan first, 235; fallacy that an author should be an actor, 235; advice to author as to man-

ager, 236; why some men of genius fail as dramatists, 237; fortunate that Dickens and Tennyson failed, 237; the only career worth having is in original work, 237; the processes of Schiller, Coleman, Garrick, and Macready, 238; trial performances not useful for a play of any value, 239; folly of beseiging managers with unsuitable plays, 239; the author the best judge of his own work, 240; folly of reading it to others promiscuously, 240; time required to write a play, 240; rarity of good or timely plays, 241; fallacy that a play cannot be judged in the reading, 241; failures sometimes accidental, 241; need to examine all criticisms, 242.

Plot, Chapter IV., 65, 72-76, 102, 228, 247, 250.

Poetic justice; see Satisfaction, and 2; 20, 93.

Pougin's Encyclopædia, 258.

Premises, must be accepted, 23, 28; for with premise, argument, conclusion, each must be convincing and logical, 65.

Preparation, the cause before the effect, of the utmost importance, 83, 84, 98, 110, 171, 175.

Present, the, is the essence of the drama, 81, 138.

Principle, the literature of dramatic, Chapter XII., 243.

Principles, the inexorable nature of, 15, 54.

Principles, a summary of certain laws in art, Chapter VII., 165; drama contains all the elements of art, 165; compared with elements of painting, 165; perspicuity, 165; intelligibility, clearness, 166; language to be dramatic, 166; language to fit character, 166; sincerity and simplicity, 167; contrast, 167; proportion, 168; Dumas *fils* places it first, 169; variety, 169; monotony, 169; variety is not discontinuity, 169; scenes not to be repeated, 169; illusion, the many dangers to, 169; author, 170; probability, 171; what is probable in one kind of play not in another, 171; illusion, 173; preparation, 174, 175; suspense, 176; "Jim the Penman," 176; more than mere curiosity, 176, 227.

Probability, 58, 171, 172.

Problem, 5, 73, 76, 92.

Progression, 1, 12, 121.

Prölls, "Geschichte des Neueren Dramas," 256.
Prologue, 87, 91, 115.
Promise, 80.
Proportion, 6, 32, 51, 57, 61, 88, 89, 96, 108, 111, 116, 123, 124, 130, 156, 164, 168; Dumas *fils* declares it to be the most important element, 169.
Purpose, essential in the drama, 111.

Racine, referred to and cited, 41, 60, 61, 126, 194, 246.
Reade, Charles, his scorn of the adapter, 181; his search for subjects, 227.
Realism, as the outward form, the incorporation, will always exist, 140, 146.
Recital, 82, 92, 111; what to be acted and what told, 114, 115, 116, 138.
"Rent Day, The," cited, 111.
Retardation, 120, 122.
"Richard III.," cited, 17, 18, 35, 90, 110, 192, 193.
"Richelieu," cited, 115, 127.
"Rivals, The," Jefferson's adaptation of, 183.
"Robbers, The," cited, 171.
Robertson, T. S., plays by, cited, 82, 101, 155, 168, 174, 182.
Rœscher, metaphysical writer on the drama, 253.
Romantic, the, 205, 210.
"Romeo and Juliet," cited, 3, 54, 88, 110, 145, 151, 157, 192, 194.
Roumien, "L'Art Dramatique," 259.
Royer, "Histoire Universelle du Théâtre," 256.
"Ruddygore," 202.
"Ruy Blas," referred to, 206.
Ryer, George W.; see "The Old Homestead," 119.

Salvini, realism in "Samson," 140.
Sanson, book on stage management, 258.
Sarcey, Francesque, his service to the drama in France, 215, 255.

Sardou, referred to and cited, 11, 32, 54, 63, 75, 82, 83, 86, 92, 95, 99, 102, 103, 106, 124, 125, 131, 135, 136, 155, 236, 255.

Satisfaction, 2, 20, 93; see Æsthetics, Character, End of Play, etc.

Scenes, Chapter V., 112; of two kinds, the picture and the action, 112; each to be significant, 112; not a scene unless it accomplishes something toward the movement, 113; organic with the play, 113; length of does not determine its value, 113; must be in the right sequence, 113; constructed, not written, 113; important for detail, 114; progressive and retroactive, 114; what to be acted, what told, 114; much to be left to actor, scenery, and public intelligence, 115; action more impressive than speech, 115; some things must be proved and hammered at possibly in words, 115; illustrated by "A Celebrated Case," 115; prologue, a bad one to "Martyr," 115; "Richelieu," 115; "The Daughter of Roland," 116; interest, 116; character may require special development in, 116; proportion, 116; effects, 116; to symbolize wherever possible, 117; value of depends on relation to other scenes, 117; "The Banker's Daughter," 117; must have purpose, 118; overwrought conversation in, evil, 118; conversation easily written, 118; author should map out before writing, 118; has its beginning, middle, and end, 119; "The Old Homestead," 119; farce comedies, 120; tableaus, 120; groups, 120; not to open with tableaus, 120; Bunn and Stanfield's conflict, 120; scenery, 120; stage not to be vacant, qualified, 120; "Faust," its scene on the Brocken, 120; pantomime is drama, 120; French definition of the acted scene, 121; its special uses as to actor, etc., 121; character in, 121; "A Scrap of Paper," 121; dialogue the greater part of a play, 121; its requirements, 121; "Antony and Cleopatra," 122; determined by character and relations, 122; authors should not speak in, 123; may be used for local color, etc., 124; uses of conversational scenes illustrated, 125; matters outside of action not to be alluded to in a play of illusion, 126;

Racine and Corneille even forbade rhetorical comparison, 126; asides, 127; necessary to mechanism, 127; monologue and soliloquy, 127; reveal emotion not to be otherwise so fully expressed, 127; peculiar also to artificial comedy, 127; when and where proper, 128; expression to be had at any cost, 128; groups peculiar to modern drama, 128; a matter of stage management, 129; necessary to historical drama, 129; episodes, 129; an interruption to the action, 130; the true and false, 130; "Julius Cæsar," 130; "The Old Homestead," 130; uses of, 130; detrimental often even if beautiful in self, 130; business, part of authorship to indicate, 131; actor entitled to freedom in methods, 131; Sardou, 131; stage-manager, his functions and methods, 132; a supplemental author, 133; scene plots, property plots, promptbook, etc., 133; significance of certain stage positions and movements, 134; Sardou's stage direction in "A Scrap of Paper," 135; desired effects the sum of the art, 135; actors' movements on the stage, 135; variety, 135; various ways of expression, 137; rising, crossing, 136; effects not to be too sudden, 136; audience to anticipate actors' movements, 136; the attention to be directed, 136; preparation, 136; scenes not to be repeated, 137; monotony, 137; an idea, however, may be played on repeatedly for distinctness, 137; effects imperative, 137; some scenes to be minute, others sketched, 137; all in a scene to be occupied or related to it, get something out of it, be helpful, etc., 138; number of persons in, dependent on object, 138; and that number affects the handling, 138; scenery should be organic with the play, 139; should not be imperfect, 139; imperfection defined and illustrated, 139; "The Lord Harry," with six hundred tons of, 139; absurdities of too much, 140; and of two frequent changes, 140; French custom, 141; front scenes, 141; scenic effect, 140; Salvini's "Samson," 140; a theory of Bronson Howard's, 141; possible and impossible, 141; tableaus, 141; illusion discussed as to change of scenery, 142; boxed interiors, 142; absurdities of modern restrictions,

143; stage management, its problems, 143; scenery necessarily subordinate to action, 144; "Elaine," 144; Shakspere's plays, with and without, 144; value of scenery, 144; "Cymbeline," 144; over-elaboration, instance of in "Romeo and Juliet," 145; realism and naturalism, 146; Henry Irving's methods, and his school of acting, 146; his management of the scene on the Brocken in "Faust," 63, 70, 147.

Schiller, referred to, plays by, cited, 11, 57, 87, 91, 171, 194, 236.

Schlegel, his "Lectures on Dramatic Art," 173, 196, 244, 252, 256.

"School," an adaptation, 182.

"School for Scandal," cited, 36, 46, 53.

Schure, Ed., book on music, 256.

Scott, Clement, his critical authority, 215.

"Scrap of Paper, A," cited, 11, 83, 86, 92, 102, 125, 135, 136, 183.

Scribe, Eugene, 194, 200.

Selby, Charles, "The Marble Heart," 82.

"Serious Family, The," referred to, 182.

Shakspere, 3, 14, 16, 17, 18, 27, 36, 41, 42, 60, 63, 65, 73, 78, 81, 82, 88, 90, 107, 110, 122, 126, 127, 130, 133, 140, 144, 145, 151, 152, 157, 158, 164, 172, 181, 189, 192, 193, 194, 205, 213, 217, 218, 226, 236, 254.

"Shenandoah," a theory of stage management in, 141.

Sheridan, cited, 36, 45, 46, 53, 97, 183, 195.

Shiel, referred to, 237.

Sidney, Sir Philip, his "Defense of Poetry," 31.

"Silver King, The," cited, 87.

Simpson, his book on the unities, 60.

Simpson, Palgrave, referred to, 183.

Situation, 96, 97, 100.

Soliloquy; see Monologue, 127.

Spectacular, the, 199.

Spectator, the; see Audience.

"Sphinx, The," cited, 38.

Spielhagen, his essays on the novel, 253.
Stage-manager, Chapter V., 112; 132–136, 143, 170.
Stanfield, scenic painter, 120.
Stock companies, the value of, 211.
Stolen and patched-up plays, 190.
"Stranger, The," cited, 23.
Subject; see Chapters I. and II.; 63.
Suggestion, as distinguished from the detail in the action and in the scenery, 137, 141.
Sulzer's "Theorie der Kunst," 252.
Suspense, an element, 11, 34, 93, 94, 99, 122, 176.
Sympathy, an element, 1, 89.

Tableaus, limitation of, 62; there should not be too much movement, but all to be effective in every detail, without confusion, as in "Faust," 147.
Taine, as a critic of the drama in history, 256.
Talfourd, referred to, 237.
"Tartuffe," the original of other plays, 182.
Taste; see Æsthetics.
Teal, his effective management of a scene, 258.
Technical, the; see Drama, the Three Elements of, Chapter II., 20, 39, 53.
Tennyson, why he failed as a writer of plays, 237.
Theatre, the, 16–19, 211.
Theatric, the, 8.
Theme, the; see Chapters I. and II., 63.
Themes, 8, 13, 103, 188.
Thomas, Augustus, author of "Alabama," 14.
Thompson, Denman, "The Old Homestead," 119, 130.
Time in the performance of play, 6.
Time, on the stage, 66–69.
Tobin, "The Honeymoon," 4.
Tolstoi, "Kreutzer Sonata," cited, 30.
Tone, a quality in a play, 89, 210.
Tragedy, 192.

Translation, often confounded with adaptation, 180, 181.
Truth, the aim of the drama, 4.
"Two Orphans, The," cited, 78, 84, 89, 109, 156, 179, 183.

"Under the Gaslight," cited, 36, 46, 53.
Unity, Chapter III., 56; definition of, 56; the organic illustrated, 56; proportion, harmony, congruity, numberless elements of, 57; affected by improbabilities, 58; divided attention, etc., 58; the three unities of the French, 59; correct within limits, 60; some absurdities of, 60; overturned by Lessing, Hugo, and others, 60; unity of action or of illusion remains, 64; is a focus of facts and interests, 63; triune unity grew out of imperfect scenery, 63; unity the logic of action and the impression of the entirety, 10, 109.

Variety, in incident, 29, 135, 169.
Vaudeville, the, 200.
"Venice Preserved," referred to, 194.
Verse, 39, 41, 42, 167, 205.
"Vicar of Wakefield," as adapted, 190.
Vice in character, 22, 26, 29, 159, 208.
Voltaire, his views and criticisms, 60, 62, 240, 246.

"Wages of Sin," referred to, 206.
Wagner, books by, 256.
"Wallenstein," love-interest in, etc., 194.
Ward's "History of the Stage," 256.
"Werther," referred to, 32.
"White Slave, The," referred to, 14.
"William Tell," early statement of certain facts in, 87.
Wills, W. G., "Olivia," 190.
Winter, William, as a critic, 215.
"Winter's Tale," cited, 164.
"Woman against Woman," cited, 206.
Writing plays; see article by W. T. Price in *North American*

Review, December, 1892; see also books and essays by Brander Mathews and Clarence Stedman.

Young, Sir Charles, play by, cited, 99, 176.

"Zaïre," time in its preparation, 240.
Zola, his excellence as a critic, etc., 146, 255.

www.ingramcontent.com/pod-product-compliance
Lightning Source LLC
Chambersburg PA
CBHW032057220426
43664CB00008B/1031